HEARTLAND COOKING

SOUPS & SALADS

Heartland Cooking
Soups & Salads

FRANCES TOWNER GIEDT

PHOTOGRAPHS BY
Eleanor Thompson

Reader's Digest

The Reader's Digest Association, Inc.
Pleasantville, New York/Montreal

A Reader's Digest Book

CONCEIVED AND PRODUCED BY
Miller and O'Shea, Inc.

DESIGNED BY
Lisa Billard Design

The acknowledgments that appear on page 5 are hereby made a part of this copyright page.

Copyright © 1996 by Miller and O'Shea, Inc.
Photography copyright © 1996 by Eleanor Thompson

Library of Congress Cataloging in Publication Data
Giedt, Frances Towner.
    Soups & salads: traditional American recipes / Frances Towner Giedt:
photographs by Eleanor Thompson.
        p.   cm.—(Heartland cooking)
    Includes index.
    ISBN 0-89577-877-7
    1. Soups. 2. Salads. 3. Cookery, American—Midwestern style.
  I. Title   II. Series.
  TX757.G54   1996
  641.8'13—dc20   96-7241

Printed in the United States of America

HEARTLAND COOKING
SOUPS & SALADS

FRANCES TOWNER GIEDT

PHOTOGRAPHS BY
Eleanor Thompson

Reader's Digest

The Reader's Digest Association, Inc.
Pleasantville, New York/Montreal

A Reader's Digest Book

CONCEIVED AND PRODUCED BY
Miller and O'Shea, Inc.

DESIGNED BY
Lisa Billard Design

The acknowledgments that appear on page 5 are hereby made a part of this copyright page.

Library of Congress Cataloging in Publication Data
Giedt, Frances Towner.
     Soups & salads: traditional American recipes / Frances Towner Giedt:
photographs by Eleanor Thompson.
          p.   cm.—(Heartland cooking)
     Includes index.
     ISBN 0-89577-877-7
     1. Soups. 2. Salads. 3. Cookery, American—Midwestern style.
  I. Title   II. Series.
  TX757.G54 1996
  641.8'13—dc20   96-7241

Printed in the United States of America

DEDICATED TO

MY BROTHER, LAILE,

AND MY SISTER, EILEEN

for helping me remember the stories

ACKNOWLEDGMENTS

THIS BOOK IS THE RESULT OF CONTRIBUTIONS BY MANY—FRIENDS, STRANGERS, FAMILY, AND colleagues—as I collected the recipes and stories.

First and foremost, great thanks to Eleanor Thompson for her always stunning photographs and to Roberta Rall, the food stylist who beautifully prepared the dishes for photography. Thanks too, to Deborah Slocomb, our prop stylist, and to Chris Hobson, a talented photo assistant.

To Coleen O'Shea and Angela Miller, who brought me the opportunity to write this book; to Kathy Kingsley and Chris Benton, whose editorial expertise polished it; and to Lisa Billard for a beautiful book design.

Gratitude goes to the many shops and stores that loaned their lovely dishes and linens for the photography of the recipes: Abbey Road Antique Market, Jenks, OK; American Hand, Westport, CT; Anthropologie, Westport, CT; The Complete Kitchen, Darien, CT; Dansk International Designs, Ltd; Eddie Bauer Home Collection; The Forgotten Garden, Wilton, CT; Full Circle Handmade Tableware, Bridgeport, CT; Hoagland's of Greenwich, Greenwich, CT; Judy Kelhoffer, Westport, CT; L.C.R., Westport, CT; Parc Monceau Country French Antiques, Westport, CT; Pier 1 Imports, Pottery Barn; Rebecca's Memories, Jenks, OK; Simon Pearce; The Wayside Exchange & Antiques, Wilton, CT; Williams-Sonoma.

This book could not have happened without the help of the agricultural departments of each of the Heartland states, which helped me research the material—they were generous with their time and willingness to answer my many questions. A special thanks also to the Cherry Marketing Institute, Inc., and the Wisconsin Milk Marketing Board.

Finally, I wish to acknowledge the ongoing support and help from my husband, David, and my family. Without their good nature and insights, this book could not have been written. I cannot thank you enough.

INTRODUCTION 8

SOUPS 11

Chicken Stock **12**

Beef Stock **13**

STARTER SOUPS 15

Chilled Carrot Bisque **16**

Cucumber Buttermilk Soup **19**

Avocado Soup **20**

Spicy Hazelnuts **21**

Country Corn Chowder **22**

Roasted Red Pepper and
Tomato Soup with Crème
Fraîche Swirl **24**

Heartland Borscht **25**

Crème Fraîche **25**

Old-Fashioned Cream of
Tomato Soup **26**

Roasted Garlic Cream Soup **28**

Cauliflower Soup **29**

Spring Asparagus and
Red Potato Soup **30**

Creamy Shiitake Mushroom
Soup **32**

Roasted Onion Soup **33**

Curried Apple Soup **34**

Pumpkin Soup **36**

Twice-Baked Potato Soup **37**

MAIN-DISH SOUPS 39

Wisconsin Cheese Chowder **41**

Whitefish Chowder **42**

Great Lakes Fish Chowder **43**

Salmon Chowder **45**

Farmers' Market Soup **46**

Garlic Croutons **47**

Pheasant Soup **49**

Chicken Spaetzle Soup **50**

Turkey Minestrone **51**

Autumn Rabbit Soup **52**

Lentil Soup **54**

Garden Beef Soup **55**

Goulash Soup **57**

Ham and Sweet Potato
Chowder **58**

Pork and Bean Soup **59**

Shrimp and Tomato Soup **61**

Velvet Chicken Soup **62**

Chili Clam Chowder **63**

Spicy Sausage Soup **64**

FRUIT SOUPS 67

Rhubarb Buttermilk Soup **68**

Blueberry-Blackberry Soup **69**

Cherry Soup **70**

Strawberry Melon Soup **72**

Peach Soup **73**

Sparkling Cranberry Soup **74**

SALADS 76

Salad Greens **77**

**VEGETABLE AND
GREEN SALADS 79**

Fruited Spinach Salad with
Poppy Seed Dressing **80**

Endive, Pear, and Blue Cheese
Salad with Balsamic
Dressing **83**

Romaine Salad with Warm
Cheese Dressing **84**

Tomato Salad with Jalapeño
Mayonnaise **85**

Molded Cucumber Salad **86**

To Unmold Gelatin Salads **87**

Warm Fiddlehead Salad **88**

Specialty Vinegars **89**

Heartland Summer Corn
and Tomato Salad **91**

ENTS

Warm Grilled Vegetable
Salad **92**

Karen's Garlicky and
Sweet Coleslaw **93**

Summer Confetti Salad **94**

Bean Medley **97**

Kansas Layered 24-Hour
Salad **98**

Old-Fashioned Red
Potato Salad **99**

North Woods Wild Rice
Salad **100**

Warm Root Vegetable Salad **101**

Beet and Apple Salad **102**

Seeding a Pomegranate **102**

Macaroni and Cheese Salad **103**

Broccoli Salad with Sweet
and Sour Raisin Dressing **105**

Mixed Grain Salad with
Feta Dressing **106**

POULTRY, SEAFOOD, AND MEAT SALADS 109

Hot German Potato Salad
with Grilled Sausages **111**

Grilled Steak and Asparagus
Salad with Cilantro
Dressing **112**

Tortilla Taco Salad **114**

Potato, Ham, and Pea Salad
with Fresh Dill **117**

BLT in a Bowl with Garlic
Croutons **119**

Roast Beef Salad **120**

Wilted Greens with Chicken
and Cranberries **121**

Grilled Duck Salad **122**

Smoked Turkey Salad **123**

Grilled Citrus Chicken
Salad **124**

Tuna and Pasta Salad **125**

Seafood Salad with White
Beans **126**

Warm Shrimp Caesar
Salad **128**

FRUIT SALADS 131

Prairie Fruit Salad **132**

Summertime Fruit Salad
with Honey-Lime
Dressing **134**

Cantaloupe, Tomato, and
Avocado Salad with
Hot Chile Dressing **135**

Mixed Fall Fruit Salad **136**

Berry and Pretzel Salad **137**

Tangy Lemon-Lime Mold **138**

Molded Waldorf Salad with
Cranberry Dressing **139**

Frozen Cranberry Snow **140**

SOURCES 142

INDEX 142

I GREW UP IN THE HEARTLAND, THE GEOGRAPHICAL CENTER OF THE UNITED STATES and the cradle of our country's farm-style cooking. Stretching from the Canadian border south to Oklahoma and reaching from Ohio to the foothills of the Rockies, the Heartland encompasses the mighty Mississippi River, the Great Lakes, and nearly twenty million acres of fertile farmland and dense forests. In the 1600s, when the French explorers traveled south from Canada looking for the northwest passage to the Orient, they planted the first cherry trees in Michigan, using cherry pits from Normandy. By the mid-19th century the vast prairies of Illinois, Indiana, and Wisconsin were producing wheat. By 1870 wheat was introduced to the grassy plains of Nebraska and Kansas.

It was fifteen years later, in 1885, that my maternal grandfather immigrated to Kansas and bought his first 160 acres of Kansas land (a wheat farm that's still in my family) for less than fifty dollars, beginning a family tradition of farming and living off the land.

Life on the prairie wasn't easy, but fresh food was abundant. In the hot summer months the family would dine on bass and

catfish from the river that flowed through the farm, fresh vegetables from the extensive kitchen garden, and wild mushrooms and watercress picked alongside the creek. Summer brought an explosion of fresh berries and currants. The branches of the apple, peach, and plum trees were heavy with fruit. Deer, pheasant, rabbit, and wild turkey were plentiful, supplementing the small herd of cows, the family of pigs, and the several varieties of chickens that inhabited the barnyard.

The harsh winters of Kansas called for substantial food — sturdy stews and savory soups to warm the body that made use of the supplies of the root cellar and the smokehouse. This tradition of cooking seasonally from the land is the essence of Heartland cooking.

No other foods change so drastically from season to season as soup and salad. In the hot summer months of the Heartland, cold soups are sparkling with flavor and come in a rainbow of colors, strewn with fresh herbs. Hot summer soups are delicate in texture, often based on light broths with bits of seafood or poultry. Summer salads

are full of vine-ripened tomatoes, vegetables still warm from the garden, tree-ripened fruits, and luscious berries.

When winter settles in, Heartlanders turn to steaming bowls of thick, stick-to-the-ribs soups and chowders, filled with meats, beans, root vegetables, and cheese to fortify everyone against the winter's chill. Salads change with the season, too. As autumn light starts to fade and the nights turn long and cold, salads change to substantial offerings of earthy grains, pasta, dried beans, and winter fruits. The addition of meat, poultry, and fish contribute to the variety. Heartland

DUCTION

salads may be side- or main-dish meals, dressed or molded dishes. Served alone or teamed with a favorite soup, this is food to satisfy hungry family and friends. In *Soups & Salads*, I offer a contemporary collection of recipes that showcases the vast Heartland's ever-expanding pantry. I hope that the recipes enhance your thinking about Midwestern food and tempt you to further explore the range of foods and produce and the interconnection of the many ethnic influences on the cuisine of the Heartland.

NUTRITIONAL INFORMATION

For these recipes the nutritional analysis uses the most current data from "The Food Processor," Version 6.02, by ESHA Research, and the United States Department of Agriculture. Nutritional information is given for calories; grams of protein, total fat and saturated fat, carbohydrates, and dietary fiber; and milligrams of sodium and cholesterol. The nutritional analysis does not include optional ingredients or those for which no specific amount is stated.

METRIC CONVERSION CHART

LIQUID AND DRY MEASURE EQUIVALENTS

Customary	Metric
¼ teaspoon	1.25 milliliters
½ teaspoon	2.5 milliliters
1 teaspoon	5 milliliters
1 tablespoon	15 milliliters
1 fluid ounce	30 milliliters
¼ cup	60 milliliters
⅓ cup	80 milliliters
½ cup	120 milliliters
1 cup	240 milliliters
1 pint (2 cups)	480 milliliters
1 quart (4 cups; 32 ounces)	960 milliliters (.35 liter)
1 gallon (4 quarts)	3.84 liters
1 ounce (by weight)	28.35 grams
¼ pound (4 ounces)	114 grams
1 pound (16 ounces)	454 grams
2.2 pounds	1 kilogram (1,000 grams)

TEMPERATURE EQUIVALENTS

Description	°Fahrenheit	°Celsius
Very cool	200–250	95–120
Cool or slow	275–300	135–150
Warm	325	165
Moderate	350	175
Moderately hot	375	190
Fairly hot	400	200
Hot	425	220
Very hot	450–475	230–245

COOKING AND BAKING EQUIVALENTS

Bakeware	Customary	Metric
Round Pan	8 x 1½ inches	20 x 4 cm
	9 x 1½ inches	23 x 4 cm
	10 x 1½ inches	25 x 4 cm
Square Pan	8 x 8 x 2 inches	20 x 20 x 5 cm
	9 x 9 x 2 inches	23 x 23 x 5 cm
Baking Dishes	7 x 11 x 1½ inches	18 x 28 x 4 cm
	7½ x 12 x 2 inches	19 x 30 x 5 cm
	9 x 13 x 2 inches	23 x 33 x 5 cm
Loaf Pan	4½ x 8½ x 2½ inches	11 x 21 x 6 cm
	5 x 9 x 3 inches	13 x 23 x 8 cm
Muffin Cups	2½ x 1¼ inches	6 x 3 cm
	3 x 1½ inches	8 x 4 cm
Casseroles and Saucepans	1 quart	1 liter
	1½ quart	1.5 liter
	2 quart	2 liter
	2½ quart	2.5 liter
	3 quart	3 liter
	4 quart	4 liter

S O U P S

ONE OF THE PLEASURES OF making soups is that they are easily concocted and the cook can show great versatility. Hot or cold, savory or sweet, chunky or smooth, soup offers an astonishing variety of flavors and textures.

All that's needed are a few familiar ingredients; a good heavy-duty soup pot; an assortment of stirring and skimming spoons; a chopping board and knife; a paring knife and potato peeler; and a strainer, sieve, or colander. A food processor will make easy work of much of the chopping, and you'll need it or a blender to puree some of the soups. When a soup contains both a dairy product and a highly acidic ingredient, such as tomatoes, it may have a tendency to curdle. To prevent this from happening, do not let the soup come to a boil once the dairy product has been added.

To serve the soup you'll need a soup ladle, some soup bowls (I prefer wide, shallow soup bowls for hearty, thick soups), and some soup spoons. You can also use oversized cups or mugs for hot soups and large, shallow glasses or crystal cups for cold soups.

Although I own a variety of soup tureens, you can also serve soup from a large crockery bowl or even a large pitcher. Since homemade soup freezes well, you'll also want to have a supply of plastic freezer containers for leftovers.

Whether it's a hearty soup sturdy enough to serve as a main dish for dinner or a light first course soup to take the edge off your appetite, most soups are usually based on a rich, savory stock. Most commercial stocks are very salty. Look for varieties labeled "low-sodium" or "no salt added" to comply with the sodium levels calculated for these recipes. Canned stock also contains a fair amount of fat. If you chill the can of stock first, you can remove and discard the fat that solidifies on the surface.

I make my own stock on days when I'm working on a project that will keep me at home most of the day. Since stock takes little attention and it freezes well, I always have a supply of chicken or beef stock on hand for making soup. You can freeze the stock in ice cube trays. Once frozen, pack the cubes of stock in a zipper-type plastic freezer bag.

CHICKEN STOCK

MAKES 3 QUARTS

A soup is only as good as the stock with which it is made. I rely heavily on this recipe for chicken stock and always have a supply in my freezer for making soups and sauces. Whenever I buy a whole chicken for cutting up into breasts, thighs, and legs, I freeze what's remaining to make stock. It doesn't take long to accumulate the necessary 3 pounds.

3 pounds chicken pieces, such as wings, necks, and backs
2 medium yellow onions, peeled and each stuck with 1 whole clove
1 large carrot, peeled and cut into 4 pieces
1 large celery rib with leaves, cut into 4 pieces

1 large garlic clove, peeled
4 quarts water
6 peppercorns
4 sprigs fresh flat-leaf parsley
1 bay leaf
1 sprig fresh thyme
¼ teaspoon salt

**PREP TIME:
15 MIN
COOK TIME:
2 3/4 HR**

1. Rinse chicken pieces and pat dry. In a 6-quart soup pot, combine chicken, onions, carrot, celery, garlic, and water. Bring to a boil over medium-high heat. Skim off and discard any foam that rises to surface. Add peppercorns, parsley, bay leaf, thyme, and salt. Reduce heat, partially cover, and simmer for 2½ hours. Occasionally skim off and discard any foam.

2. Strain stock into a large bowl through a fine sieve or colander lined with cheesecloth; discard solids. Refrigerate warm stock, uncovered, until thoroughly chilled. Discard any fat that rises and solidifies on the surface.

3. Store in a sealed container in refrigerator for up to 3 days or freeze for up to 3 months. Makes about twelve 1-cup servings.

One 1-cup serving: 13 calories, trace protein, trace total fat (0 saturated), 3 g carbohydrates, 46 mg sodium, 0 cholesterol, trace dietary fiber

BEEF STOCK

MAKES 2 QUARTS

Roasting the bones and vegetables adds a rich flavor to this stock. Ask the butcher to crack the bones to extract more flavor and nutrients into the liquid.

5 pounds mixed beef and veal bones, such as marrow, knuckle, and shin	1 leek, white part only, well rinsed and cut into 4 pieces
2 large yellow onions, peeled and cut in half	1 large garlic clove, peeled
2 large carrots, peeled and cut into 4 pieces	6 quarts water
2 large celery ribs with leaves, cut into 4 pieces	8 peppercorns
	6 sprigs fresh flat-leaf parsley
	5 sprigs fresh thyme
	1 large bay leaf

**PREP TIME:
15 MIN + 1 HR
TO ROAST BONES
AND VEGETABLES

COOK TIME:
6 3/4 HR**

1. Preheat oven to 400°F. Put bones in a single layer in a large roasting pan. Scatter onions, carrots, celery, leek, and garlic around the bones. Roast, uncovered, for 1 hour, until bones and vegetables begin to brown.

2. Transfer bones and vegetables to a 6-quart soup pot. Add water and bring to a boil over medium-high heat. Skim off and discard any foam that rises to surface. Add peppercorns, parsley, thyme, and bay leaf. Reduce heat and simmer, uncovered, for 6 hours. Occasionally skim off and discard any foam.

3. Strain stock into a large bowl through a fine sieve or a colander lined with cheesecloth; discard solids. Return stock to pot and simmer, uncovered, until reduced to 2 quarts, about 30 minutes.

4. Refrigerate warm stock, uncovered, until thoroughly chilled. Discard any fat that rises and solidifies on the surface.

5. Store in a sealed container in refrigerator for up to 3 days or freeze for up to 3 months. Makes about eight 1-cup servings.

One 1-cup serving: 36 calories, 2 g protein, trace total fat (trace saturated), 8 g carbohydrates, 48 mg sodium, 0 cholesterol, 1 g dietary fiber

STARTER SOUPS

WHETHER FOR AN INFORMAL family meal or a very special sit-down dinner for friends, I frequently opt for soup as the first course. Since most soups taste even better the next day, I can make the soup ahead of time. If the main course is rich, I serve a light soup to stimulate the appetite; if the main course is light, I serve a more sturdy soup to round out the meal.

Here you'll find a rainbow of choices from the ruby-red Heartland Borscht and the vibrant Avocado Soup to begin a warm-weather meal on a festive note, or when the cold wind's blowing, try the Roasted Onion Soup or Twice-Baked Potato Soup.

To serve a first course soup with style, look around for soup bowls with unusual shapes; wide, shallow bowls with great rims; shallow clear bowls or short-stemmed goblets that will let chilled soup sparkle; or maybe don't even use a bowl at all— hollowed-out bell peppers or small squash and pumpkins can make terrific, fanciful containers for soup. Don't forget the garnish to complement the appearance and heighten the flavor of the soup.

CHILLED CARROT BISQUE

Like other working women, I have limited time for preparing day-to-day meals. So when my market started offering bags of already-peeled baby carrots at a reasonable price, I felt like celebrating. The little finger-size carrots are particularly sweet and make an excellent soup to serve icy cold.

2 tablespoons butter
8 shallots, minced (½ cup)
1 16-ounce package peeled fresh
   baby carrots (3 cups)
3 cups chicken stock (page 12)
   or canned low-sodium broth
1 sprig fresh thyme or ¼ teaspoon
   dried, crumbled

1 ½ cups unsweetened pineapple juice
   Salt, optional, and freshly ground
   black pepper to taste
   Sour cream for garnish, optional
   Sprigs fresh mint for garnish, optional

PREP TIME: 10 MIN
COOK TIME: 40 MIN
CHILL TIME: AT LEAST 4 HR

1. In a 3-quart saucepan, melt butter over medium heat. Add shallots and sauté until soft, about 5 minutes. Add carrots, stock, and thyme and bring to a boil over medium-high heat. Reduce the heat, cover, and simmer until carrots are very tender, about 30 minutes. If using fresh thyme, remove and discard.

2. In a food processor or blender, puree the soup in batches. Transfer the soup to a large bowl. Stir in pineapple juice. Taste and add salt and pepper. Cover and chill for at least 4 hours or overnight.

3. To serve, stir well before ladling into soup bowls. Garnish each serving with a dollop of sour cream and a sprig of fresh mint. Makes about six 1-cup servings.

1 serving: 114 calories, 1 g protein, 4 g total fat (2.5 g saturated), 19 g carbohydrates, 91 mg sodium, 10 mg cholesterol, 3 g dietary fiber

CUCUMBER BUTTERMILK SOUP

I've been making this refreshing soup for years. It is the perfect first course when the weather is warm. There is no substitute for the fresh mint. It's easy to grow fresh mint. But if you don't wish to do so, it is available in most supermarkets year-round.

2 medium cucumbers, peeled
2 shallots, minced (2 tablespoons)
1 large garlic clove, minced
2 cups low-fat (1.5%) buttermilk
1 ¾ cups chicken stock (page 13) or canned low-sodium broth
¼ cup lightly packed fresh mint leaves, minced

1 tablespoon fresh lemon juice
Salt, optional, and freshly ground black pepper to taste
Paper-thin slices of unpeeled cucumber for garnish, optional
Sprigs fresh mint for garnish, optional
Grated lemon rind for garnish, optional

PREP TIME: 20 MIN

CHILL TIME: AT LEAST 4 HR

1. Slice cucumbers in half lengthwise. Using a small spoon, scoop out and discard cucumber seeds. Using a food processor or hand grater, coarsely grate cucumbers.
2. In a large bowl, combine cucumbers, shallots, garlic, buttermilk, stock, mint, and lemon juice. Taste and add salt, if desired, and pepper. Cover and chill for at least 4 hours or overnight.
3. To serve, stir well before ladling into soup bowls. Garnish each serving with a few slices of cucumber, a sprig of mint, and a sprinkling of grated lemon rind. Makes about four 1¼-cup servings.

1 serving: 80 calories, 5 g protein, 1 g total fat (0.7 g saturated), 12 g carbohydrates, 160 mg sodium, 4 mg cholesterol, 1 g dietary fiber

AVOCADO SOUP

MAKES 6 SERVINGS

Like the rest of the country, Heartlanders have become addicted to the rich taste and buttery texture of the avocado. When I was growing up in Kansas, avocados were available on a very limited basis and quite expensive. Today they are available in even the smallest grocery stores. On a recent trek through the Missouri Ozarks, I enjoyed a delicious chilled avocado soup at a farmhouse luncheonette. The soup was the essence of avocado sprinkled with an ingenious garnish of crumbled crisp bacon and spicy hazelnuts. After several attempts to re-create this soup in my own kitchen, I've come up with this combination that would be wonderful served before a main course of grilled fish or chicken. If you are concerned about fat grams, you can use milk in place of the half-and-half, but the soup will be less creamy.

3 large ripe avocados, preferably Hass, pitted, peeled, and cut into large chunks
3 tablespoons fresh lemon juice
1 large garlic clove, minced
   About 3 cups chicken stock (page 12) or canned low-sodium broth

1 small white onion, peeled and cut into quarters
½ cup half-and-half
   Salt, optional, and freshly ground black pepper to taste
3 slices bacon, crisply cooked, drained, and crumbled for garnish, optional

**PREP TIME:
20 MIN
CHILL TIME:
AT LEAST 4 HR**

1. In a food processor or blender, combine avocados, lemon juice, and garlic and process until finely chopped. Add 2 cups stock and the onion. Process for 15 seconds, until onion is minced.
2. Transfer mixture to a large nonreactive bowl and whisk in half-and-half and up to 1 cup additional stock until soup is desired consistency. Cover tightly and chill for at least 4 hours or overnight.
3. To serve, stir soup well. Taste and add salt, if desired, and pepper. Ladle into small chilled soup bowls or cups and garnish each serving with a sprinkling of crumbled bacon and the hazelnuts. Makes about six ⅔-cup servings.

1 serving: 315 calories, 5 g protein, 29 g total fat (7.3 g saturated), 13 g carbohydrates, 132 mg sodium, 20 mg cholesterol, 5 g dietary fiber

SPICY HAZELNUTS

MAKES ½ CUP

2 tablespoons butter
½ cup coarsely chopped hazelnuts
¼ teaspoon dried oregano leaves, crumbled
⅛ teaspoon dried thyme leaves, crumbled
⅛ teaspoon ground cumin
⅛ teaspoon cayenne pepper

In a nonstick skillet, melt butter over medium heat. Add hazelnuts, oregano, thyme, cumin, and cayenne. Stir until nuts are toasted, about 5 minutes. Remove from heat and set aside.

1 tablespoon: 85 calories, 1 g protein, 9 g total fat (2.2 g saturated), 2 g carbohydrates, 99 mg sodium, 8 mg cholesterol, 1 g dietary fiber

COUNTRY CORN CHOWDER

MAKES 8 SERVINGS

In the Rodgers and Hammerstein musical Oklahoma! *the hero sings about corn "as high as an elephant's eye." That's how I perceived corn to be when I was playing hide-and-seek in my father's Kansas cornfields. Since corn begins to turn to starch the moment it's plucked from the stalk, my mother would always have the pot of water boiling before someone was dispatched to pick the corn. Nothing compares to the sweet taste of fresh-picked corn— it's worth the effort to find a market where it is delivered from farms daily.*

2 tablespoons olive oil
1 large yellow onion, finely chopped (1 ½ cups)
2 medium celery ribs, chopped (1 cup)
1 large garlic clove, minced
6 large ears fresh-picked white or yellow corn
1 large yellow bell pepper, seeded and chopped (1 ½ cups)
2 jalapeño chile peppers, seeded and chopped (¼ cup)

6 cups chicken stock (page 12) or canned low-sodium broth
2 small thin-skinned potatoes, scrubbed and sliced (1 cup)
Salt, optional, and freshly ground black pepper to taste
2 large plum tomatoes, chopped (1 cup)
½ cup shredded Cheddar cheese (2 ounces) for garnish, optional
⅓ cup loosely packed fresh cilantro leaves for garnish, optional

PREP TIME: 45 MIN
COOK TIME: 35 MIN

1. In a 4-quart soup pot, heat oil over medium heat. Add onion, celery, and garlic and sauté until vegetables are soft but not browned, about 5 minutes.
2. Meanwhile, remove the husks and silk from the corn. Hold each cob vertically over a shallow dish and, using a sharp knife, cut the kernels from the cob. (You will have about 4 cups of kernels.)
3. Add half of the corn kernels and the peppers to the pot and sauté for 5 minutes. Add stock and potatoes and bring to a boil over medium-high heat. Reduce the heat, cover, and simmer for 15 minutes. Taste and add salt, if desired, and pepper.
4. Stir in tomatoes and remaining corn. Simmer, uncovered, until heated through, about 5 minutes.
5. To serve, ladle into soup bowls and garnish each serving with shredded cheese and a few cilantro leaves. Makes about eight 1 ½-cup servings.

1 serving: 174 calories, 6 g protein, 7 g total fat (2.1 g saturated), 26 g carbohydrates, 107 mg sodium, 7 mg cholesterol, 4 g dietary fiber

ROASTED RED PEPPER AND TOMATO SOUP WITH CRÈME FRAÎCHE SWIRL

MAKES 6 SERVINGS

On my travels through the Heartland one summer, I stopped in Tulsa, Oklahoma, to visit friends. Early Saturday morning my hostess insisted on taking me to the farmers' market in nearby Bixby. I came away with several grocery sacks of produce still warm from the fields, including a large bag of vine-ripened tomatoes. Roasting them for this soup enhanced their farm-fresh flavor. The crème fraîche is a wonderful tart topping, richer than sour cream, and makes a delicious addition to this soup. Use any leftover crème fraîche as a topping for pancakes, waffles, or any dessert. It takes thirty-six hours to make, so plan ahead. You can also look for ready-made crème fraîche at larger supermarkets, or use sour cream.

3 large red bell peppers, halved
   lengthwise and seeded
3 large tomatoes, cored and halved
2 tablespoons olive oil
2 medium red onions,
   chopped (2 cups)
1 large garlic clove, minced

3 cups chicken stock (page 12) or
   canned low-sodium broth
   Salt, optional, and freshly ground
   black pepper to taste
6 tablespoons crème fraîche (recipe follows)
2 tablespoons chopped fresh chives
   for garnish, optional

PREP TIME: 40 MIN + 36 HR TO MAKE CRÈME FRAÎCHE

COOK TIME: 35 MIN

1. Preheat broiler. Place peppers and tomatoes, cut sides down, on a large baking sheet. Broil 4 inches from the heat source until skins are charred and blistered, about 10 minutes. Transfer peppers to a plastic or brown paper bag, seal, and let stand for 10 to 15 minutes. Let tomatoes cool on baking sheet. When cool enough to handle, peel tomatoes using a small, sharp knife and coarsely chop. Peel skins from peppers and coarsely chop.

2. In a 4-quart soup pot, heat oil over medium-low heat. Add onions and garlic and sauté until onions are soft, about 5 minutes. Add roasted peppers and tomatoes and stock. Bring to a boil over medium-high heat. Reduce the heat, cover, and simmer, stirring occasionally, for 25 minutes.

3. In a food processor or blender, puree the soup in batches. Return soup to pan and bring to a boil over medium-high heat, stirring often. Taste and add salt, if desired, and pepper.

4. To serve, ladle into soup bowls. Place a tablespoon of crème fraîche in the center of each serving and swirl with the tip of a knife. Garnish with chopped chives. Makes about six 1½-cup servings.

1 serving (with 1 tablespoon crème fraîche): 153 calories, 3 g protein, 9 g total fat (3.4 g saturated), 17 g carbohydrates, 41 mg sodium, 13 mg cholesterol, 4 g dietary fiber

HEARTLAND BORSCHT

MAKES 4 SERVINGS

Heartlanders of Eastern European heritage enjoy this soup in the middle of the summer when the garden's producing tiny, tender beets, about 1 ½ inches in diameter. The ruby red soup turns pink as the sour cream mixes in.

1 pound small fresh beets, scrubbed and trimmed
¼ teaspoon salt
Freshly ground black pepper to taste
¼ cup red wine vinegar
2 medium carrots, peeled and diced (1 ½ cups)
2 medium leeks, white part only, well rinsed and chopped (1 cup)

1 large garlic clove, minced
1 quart chicken stock (page 12) or canned low-sodium broth
1 small head green cabbage (about ½ pound), finely shredded (2 cups)
⅓ cup sour cream or crème fraîche (recipe follows) for garnish, optional
4 sprigs fresh dill for garnish, optional

PREP TIME: 35 MIN
COOK TIME: 35 MIN
CHILL TIME: AT LEAST 4 HR

1. In a medium bowl, cover beets with boiling water and let stand for 1 minute. Drain well. Peel and coarsely grate beets. Season with salt (to set color) and pepper. In a small bowl, combine ½ cup grated beets and the vinegar. Set aside.

2. In a 4-quart soup pot, combine carrots, leeks, garlic, and stock. Bring to a boil over medium-high heat. Reduce heat, cover, and simmer for 10 minutes. Add remaining beets, cover, and simmer until vegetables are tender, about 15 minutes. Add cabbage, cover, and simmer for 5 minutes. Remove from heat.

3. Transfer soup to a large nonreactive bowl and stir in reserved beets; let cool. Cover and chill for at least 4 hours or overnight.

4. To serve, stir well before ladling into soup bowls. Garnish each serving with a dollop of sour cream and a sprig of fresh dill. Makes about four 2-cup servings.

1 serving: 149 calories, 4 g protein, 4 g total fat (2.6 g saturated), 26 g carbohydrates, 306 mg sodium, 9 mg cholesterol, 5 g dietary fiber

CRÈME FRAÎCHE

MAKES 2 CUPS

1 cup heavy cream
1 cup sour cream

In a small bowl, whisk heavy cream and sour cream until well blended. Cover and let stand in a warm place for 12 hours. Stir and chill for 24 hours before using.

1 tablespoon: 41 calories, trace protein, 4 g total fat (2.7 g saturated)
1 g carbohydrates, 7 mg sodium, 13 mg cholesterol, 0 dietary fiber

OLD-FASHIONED CREAM OF TOMATO SOUP

MAKES 6 SERVINGS

This warming soup was a childhood favorite of mine, a cure-all for everything from the winter blues to a stuffy cold. My mother usually made this with home-canned tomatoes, but I like it even better using vine-ripened tomatoes still warm from my garden.

5 tablespoons butter, at room temperature
2 medium yellow onions, finely chopped (2 cups)
2 medium celery ribs, thinly sliced (1 cup)
8 large ripe tomatoes, peeled and coarsely chopped (about 3 pounds), or 2 35-ounce cans whole tomatoes, undrained

1 tablespoon light brown sugar
Salt, optional, and freshly ground black pepper to taste
3 tablespoons unbleached all-purpose flour
3 cups whole milk
Snipped fresh chives for garnish, optional

PREP TIME: 10 MIN
COOK TIME: 55 MIN

1. In a 4-quart nonreactive soup pot, melt 2 tablespoons butter over low heat. Add onions and celery and sauté until onions are very soft but not browned, about 10 minutes.

2. Add tomatoes with their juice and brown sugar. Season with salt, if desired, and pepper. Cover and cook over medium heat until tomatoes are tender, about 30 minutes.

3. In a medium bowl, mix the remaining 3 tablespoons butter and the flour. Whisk in 1 cup hot soup, then whisk the flour mixture into the soup. Bring mixture to a boil over medium-high heat. Reduce the heat and simmer, uncovered, stirring occasionally, until soup is thickened, about 10 minutes.

4. Meanwhile, in a medium saucepan, heat milk over medium heat until it almost reaches the boiling point. Add hot milk to soup and stir until well blended. Heat until steaming but not boiling.

5. To serve, ladle into soup bowls or mugs. Garnish each serving with snipped chives. Makes about six 1 ½-cup servings.

1 serving: 254 calories, 7 g protein, 15 g total fat (8.7 g saturated), 27 g carbohydrates, 199 mg sodium, 42 mg cholesterol, 4 g dietary fiber

ROASTED GARLIC CREAM SOUP

MAKES 8 SERVINGS

Midwesterners are fond of roasted garlic. On more than one occasion in a Heartland restaurant, I have been offered whole roasted heads of garlic for plucking out the savory cloves to spread on wedges of thick toast. The roasting tames the raw, pungent flavor of the garlic, making it mellow and sweet. Here it's the base for a garlicky cream soup that tastes purely divine. The garlic takes an hour to roast and can be made earlier in the day or even the day before. The rest of the soup goes together quickly. Plan your meal accordingly since the soup needs to be served immediately once made. This is a terrific soup to offer as a first course when you're serving roasted meat, fish, or fowl.

4 heads garlic (about ½ pound)
¼ cup olive oil
3 tablespoons butter
4 medium leeks, white part only, well rinsed and chopped (2 cups)
3 tablespoons unbleached all-purpose flour
5 cups chicken stock (page 12) or canned low-sodium broth

1 medium thin-skinned potato, peeled and diced (1 cup)
1 cup heavy cream
Salt, optional, and freshly ground black pepper to taste
Chopped fresh parsley for garnish, optional

PREP TIME: 15 MIN + 1 HR TO ROAST GARLIC
COOK TIME: 50 MIN

1. Preheat oven to 350°F. Line a baking sheet with aluminum foil. Cut off ¼ inch from the top of each head of garlic. Put garlic heads, cut sides up, on prepared baking sheet and drizzle with olive oil. Bake until golden and very soft, about 1 hour. Cool slightly, then squeeze the pulp from each garlic clove. Discard the papery skins and chop the garlic pulp.

2. In a 3-quart saucepan, melt butter over medium heat. Add roasted garlic and leeks and sauté until leeks are soft, about 5 minutes. Reduce heat to low and sprinkle with flour. Cook, stirring frequently, for 10 minutes. Add stock and potato and bring to a boil over medium-high heat. Reduce heat and simmer, uncovered, until potatoes are tender, about 20 minutes.

3. In a food processor or blender, puree the soup in batches. Return soup to pan and whisk in heavy cream until well blended. Simmer, uncovered, for 10 minutes more. Do not allow the soup to come to a boil. Taste and add salt, if desired, and pepper.

4. To serve, ladle into soup bowls and garnish each serving with chopped parsley. Makes about eight 1-cup servings.

1 serving: 287 calories, 3 g protein, 22 g total fat (10.5 g saturated), 20 g carbohydrates, 95 mg sodium, 52 mg cholesterol, 2 g dietary fiber

CAULIFLOWER SOUP

MAKES 8 SERVINGS

The Jolly Green Giant is from Minnesota. It all began in 1903 when the Minnesota Valley Farming Company was founded and began selling canned vegetables. The company trademark, the familiar green man in a suit of leaves, was born twenty years later, and in 1950 the company officially became the Green Giant Company. Every year this Heartland company processes millions of tons of canned and frozen vegetables.

2 tablespoons butter

1 large yellow onion, chopped (1 ½ cups)

3 small thin-skinned potatoes, scrubbed and diced (1 ½ cups)

1 large celery rib with leaves, chopped (1 ⅓ cups)

1 large cauliflower (about 2 pounds), broken into florets, or 2 10-ounce packages frozen cauliflower

6 cups chicken stock (page 12) or canned low-sodium broth

1 sprig fresh thyme or ¼ teaspoon dried, crumbled

1 cup half-and-half
    Salt, optional, and freshly ground black pepper to taste
    Chopped fresh parsley for garnish, optional

PREP TIME: 20 MIN
COOK TIME: 35 MIN

1. In a 4-quart soup pot, melt butter over medium heat. Add onion, potatoes, and celery and sauté until vegetables are soft, about 10 minutes. Add cauliflower, stock, and thyme and bring to a boil over medium-high heat. Reduce heat, cover, and simmer until cauliflower is tender, about 15 minutes (if using frozen cauliflower, simmer for about 10 minutes).

2. In a food processor or blender, puree soup in batches. Return soup to pan and stir in half-and-half until well blended. Taste and add salt, if desired, and pepper. Heat until steaming but not boiling. If using fresh thyme, remove and discard.

3. To serve, ladle into soup bowls and garnish each serving with chopped parsley. Makes about eight 1 ½-cup servings.

1 serving: 126 calories, 3 g protein, 7 g total fat (4.0 g saturated), 15 g carbohydrates, 113 mg sodium, 19 mg cholesterol, 2 g dietary fiber

SPRING ASPARAGUS AND RED POTATO SOUP

MAKES 8 SERVINGS

Wild asparagus used to grow alongside a creek that meandered through one of my family's Kansas farms. I'd like to think that the fat stalks were volunteers from an abandoned patch of my grandmother's, but their presence was more likely due to the birds. Anyway, the wild asparagus was exceptionally tasty—excellent for soup. Lace the finished soup with shavings of Parmesan cheese. If you don't have a hand grater, you can make the shavings with a vegetable peeler.

2 pounds fresh asparagus spears
2 tablespoons butter
1 medium yellow onion, thinly sliced (1 ½ cups)
1 medium leek, white part only, well rinsed and thinly sliced (½ cup)
3 small red-skinned potatoes, scrubbed and diced (1 ½ cups)

6 cups chicken stock (page 12) or canned low-sodium broth
½ cup dry white wine or additional stock
1 teaspoon fresh thyme leaves or ¼ teaspoon dried, crumbled
   Salt, optional, and freshly ground black pepper to taste
3 ounces Parmesan cheese in 1 piece

**PREP TIME: 20 MIN
COOK TIME: 30 MIN**

1. Break off and discard white ends of asparagus. Cut spears into 1-inch pieces. Set aside.

2. In a 4-quart soup pot, melt butter over medium heat. Add onion and leek and sauté until onions are soft, about 5 minutes. Add potatoes, stock, wine, and thyme. Bring mixture to a boil over medium-high heat. Reduce heat, cover, and simmer for 10 minutes. Add asparagus and simmer, uncovered, for 5 to 10 minutes more, until asparagus and potatoes are tender. Taste and add salt, if desired, and pepper.

3. To serve, ladle into wide, shallow soup bowls and shave the Parmesan cheese over each serving. Makes about eight 1 ½-cup servings.

1 serving: 147 calories, 7 g protein, 6 g total fat (3.6 g saturated), 16 g carbohydrates, 241 mg sodium, 15 mg cholesterol, 3 g dietary fiber

CREAMY SHIITAKE MUSHROOM SOUP

MAKES 8 SERVINGS

Once grown only in Asia, shiitake mushrooms are now cultivated in the Heartland. Mushroom farmers in Indiana, Michigan, Minnesota, Missouri, and Wisconsin ship fresh shiitakes to supermarkets all around the country. Some farmers sell their mushrooms directly by mail order (see Sources, page 142). If shiitakes are not available, other fresh wild mushrooms such as chanterelles, morels, porcini, or portobellos can be used. A cultivated button mushroom will make a nice soup, but it simply will not have the same depth of flavor.

1 pound fresh shiitake mushrooms, cleaned
1 tablespoon fresh lemon juice
2 tablespoons butter
3 shallots, minced (3 tablespoons)
1 large garlic clove, minced
1 teaspoon fresh thyme leaves or ¼ teaspoon dried, crumbled

6 cups chicken stock (page 12) or canned low-sodium broth
1 tablespoon cornstarch dissolved in 2 tablespoons cold water
2 large plum tomatoes, chopped (1 cup)
2 cups half-and-half
Salt, optional, and freshly ground black pepper to taste

PREP TIME: 20 MIN
COOK TIME: 1 HR

1. Remove mushroom stems and set aside. Slice enough of the mushroom caps to equal 1 cup. Sprinkle with lemon juice and set aside. Coarsely chop remaining mushroom caps and reserved stems.

2. In a 4-quart soup pot, melt 1 tablespoon butter over medium heat. Add shallots and garlic and sauté until shallots are soft, about 5 minutes. Add thyme and chopped mushrooms and sauté until the liquid has evaporated, about 10 minutes. Add stock and bring to a boil over medium-high heat. Reduce heat and simmer mixture, uncovered, for 20 minutes. Whisk in dissolved cornstarch and simmer, stirring occasionally, for 10 minutes, until thickened slightly.

3. Meanwhile, in a medium skillet, melt the remaining 1 tablespoon butter over medium heat. Add reserved sliced mushrooms and sauté until just tender, about 2 minutes. Remove from heat and set aside.

4. Add tomatoes to the soup and simmer for 5 minutes. Stir in half-and-half until well blended. Simmer, stirring occasionally, until soup is steaming but not boiling. Taste and add salt, if desired, and pepper.

5. To serve, ladle into wide, shallow soup bowls and garnish each serving with sautéed mushroom slices. Makes about eight 1¼-cup servings.

1 serving: 167 calories, 3 g protein, 10 g total fat (6.2 g saturated), 18 g carbohydrates, 92 mg sodium, 30 mg cholesterol, 2 g dietary fiber

ROASTED ONION SOUP

MAKES 6 SERVINGS

Onions have been a staple in Heartland kitchens since the settlers unpacked their covered wagons. There's hardly a soup or stew made here that doesn't contain them. For this savory soup the onions are first oven-roasted, and then the assembled soup bakes in the oven. If you have a pretty oven-to-table casserole, here is a good opportunity to use it. Traditionally, Swiss cheese and bread are served in onion soup. For a change of pace I've placed thin slices of a domestic Brie cheese in the bottom of each bowl. When the soup is ladled in, the Brie will melt, adding a delightful flavor. Several cheese factories in Wisconsin make an excellent Brie.

¼ cup olive oil
1 large white onion, thinly sliced (1 ½ cups)
1 large yellow onion, thinly sliced (1 ½ cups)
4 large leeks, white part only, well rinsed and cut in half lengthwise
8 shallots, thinly sliced (¾ cup)
6 large garlic cloves, thinly sliced

Salt, optional, and freshly ground black pepper to taste
2 large plum tomatoes, thinly sliced (1 cup)
1 teaspoon fresh thyme leaves or ¼ teaspoon dried, crumbled
6 cups beef stock (page 13) or canned low-sodium broth
3 ounces Brie cheese, rind removed and thinly sliced

PREP TIME: 20 MIN
COOK TIME: 1 1/2 HR

1. Preheat oven to 500°F. Line a large baking sheet with foil. Brush with 2 tablespoons oil. Arrange onions, leeks, shallots, and garlic in a single layer on prepared baking sheet. Season with salt, if desired, and pepper. Drizzle with remaining oil. Bake until onions are tender and edges begin to brown, about 20 minutes. Remove from oven and reduce the temperature to 300°F.

2. Transfer onion mixture to a 4-quart ovenproof casserole. Top with tomato slices and thyme. Pour in stock and bake, uncovered, for 1 hour.

3. To serve, arrange 2 or 3 thin slices of Brie cheese in each soup bowl before ladling in the hot soup. Makes about six 1½-cup servings.

1 serving: 243 calories, 7 g protein, 13 g total fat (3.7 g saturated), 26 g carbohydrates, 155 mg sodium, 14 mg cholesterol, 4 g dietary fiber

CURRIED APPLE SOUP

The Midwest is apple country, with apple fairs and festivals scheduled in almost every state each fall to celebrate the harvest. The sweet-tart taste of apples has an affinity for the pungent flavor of curry. You can adjust the "heat" of this soup by adding or reducing the amount of curry powder to suit your taste. Serve this soup with roasted pork, ham, or a roasted chicken or turkey.

3 tablespoons butter
3 medium celery ribs, chopped (1 ½ cups)
1 small white onion, chopped (½ cup)
1 medium leek, white part only, well rinsed and chopped (½ cup)
2 tablespoons unbleached all-purpose flour
1 tablespoon curry powder or to taste
6 cups chicken stock (page 12) or canned low-sodium broth

4 tart apples such as Granny Smith, Mutsu, or McIntosh, peeled, cored, and sliced (4 cups)
½ cup heavy cream
¼ cup roasted sunflower seeds for garnish, optional
Thin apple slices for garnish, optional
Fresh cilantro leaves for garnish, optional

PREP TIME: 20 MIN
COOK TIME: 45 MIN

1. In a 4-quart soup pot, melt butter over medium heat. Add celery, onion, and leek and sauté until vegetables are soft but not browned, about 5 minutes. Using a slotted spoon, remove vegetables and set aside.

2. Stir flour and curry powder into pan drippings. Whisk in 2 cups stock until well blended. Add remaining stock, reserved vegetables, and sliced apples. Bring to a boil over medium-high heat. Reduce heat, cover, and simmer for 30 minutes.

3. In a food processor or blender, puree soup in batches. Return soup to pan and whisk in heavy cream until well blended. Heat just until steaming but not boiling.

4. To serve, ladle into soup bowls and garnish each serving with sunflower seeds, apple slices, and a few cilantro leaves. Makes about eight 1-cup servings.

1 serving: 178 calories, 2 g protein, 13 g total fat (6.4 g saturated), 16 g carbohydrates, 106 mg sodium, 32 mg cholesterol, 2 g dietary fiber

PUMPKIN SOUP

MAKES 6 SERVINGS

In the early days, pumpkins were an important food in the Heartland, roasted in the ashes of the hearth, then served sweetened with maple syrup and butter. Today many apple farms in the area grow and sell pumpkins in the fall. This pumpkin soup has a wonderful smooth texture and rich flavor. Serve it when there's a snap of fall in the air and you know winter's not far behind.

1 tablespoon olive oil
2 medium leeks, white part only, well rinsed and chopped (1 cup)
1 medium yellow onion, chopped (1 cup)
1 pound thin-skinned potatoes, peeled and diced (3 ½ cups)
1 quart chicken stock (page 12) or canned low-sodium broth
½ cup dry white wine or additional stock

1 teaspoon fresh thyme leaves or ¼ teaspoon dried, crumbled
1 bay leaf
⅛ teaspoon ground nutmeg
1 16-ounce can pumpkin (about 2 cups)
Sour cream for garnish, optional
Cracked black peppercorns for garnish, optional
Sprigs fresh thyme for garnish, optional

PREP TIME: 20 MIN
COOK TIME: 35 MIN

1. In a 4-quart soup pot, heat oil over medium heat. Add leeks and onion and sauté until soft, about 5 minutes. Add potatoes, stock, wine, thyme, bay leaf, and nutmeg. Bring mixture to a boil over medium-high heat. Reduce the heat, partially cover, and simmer until potatoes are very tender, about 20 minutes. Discard bay leaf.
2. In a food processor or blender, puree mixture in batches. Return soup to pan. Stir in pumpkin until well blended. Heat until steaming but not boiling.
3. To serve, ladle into soup bowls or mugs. Garnish each serving with a dollop of sour cream, a pinch of cracked peppercorns, and a sprig of fresh thyme. Makes about six 1½-cup servings.

1 serving: 158 calories, 3 g protein, 3 g total fat, (0.5 g saturated), 29 g carbohydrates, 45 mg sodium, 0 cholesterol, 4 g dietary fiber

TWICE-BAKED POTATO SOUP

MAKES 6 SERVINGS

This recipe comes from Sue Steinman who lives in a suburb of Detroit, Michigan. She's a terrific cook who also happens to be my son Brian's mother-in-law. When Sue gave me the recipe, she confessed she frequently makes extra mashed potatoes for dinner so she'll be obliged to make this soup the next day. Loaded with flavor, this soup truly gives the humble potato star status. Colby cheese is a soft, mild flavored Cheddar cheese that was developed by Joseph Steinwald, whose father had a cheese factory near the town of Colby, Wisconsin. Its high moisture content makes it a superb cheese for cooking because it melts smoothly.

6 small red-skinned potatoes, scrubbed (about ¾ pound)

4 slices bacon, cut into ½-inch pieces

3 green onions, white part and 2 inches green tops, thinly sliced (½ cup)

2 cups whole milk

1 cup chicken stock (page 12) or canned low-sodium broth

1 cup mashed potatoes, at room temperature

¼ pound Colby cheese, cut into ½-inch cubes (1 ½ cups)

3 ounces fully cooked smoked ham, cut into ½-inch cubes (½ cup)

Salt, optional, and freshly ground black pepper to taste

PREP TIME: 20 MIN

COOK TIME: 50 MIN

1. Boil the potatoes in water to cover until tender, about 10 minutes. Drain well and set aside.

2. Meanwhile, in a 3-quart saucepan, cook bacon pieces over medium heat until crisp. Using a slotted spoon, remove to paper towels to drain. Set aside.

3. In same pan, sauté green onions in bacon drippings until soft, about 5 minutes. Drain excess fat from pan. Whisk in milk, stock, and mashed potatoes. Stir in cheese. Cook over low heat, stirring constantly, until cheese melts.

4. Slice the red potatoes. Add the potatoes and ham to soup. Taste and add salt, if desired, and pepper. Simmer, uncovered, for 15 to 20 minutes.

5. To serve, ladle into soup bowls and garnish each serving with reserved bacon pieces. Makes about six 1 ½-cup servings.

1 serving: 260 calories, 13 g protein, 14 g total fat (7.7 g saturated), 22 g carbohydrates, 521 mg sodium, 42 mg cholesterol, 2 g dietary fiber

MAIN·DISH SOUPS

AS A WHEAT FARMER'S WIFE, MY grandmother would serve a noon meal of meat or chicken, a crock full of mashed potatoes, and bowls of fresh garden vegetables and stewed fruits—sturdy food to prepare everyone for an afternoon working in the fields. Soup was most likely served as an afternoon snack or late in the day after the evening chores were done. Today, however, versatile soups are often served as a meal in themselves. Teamed with a leafy green salad and some fresh fruit, soup makes a lovely evening meal.

A main-dish soup can also be the center of a casual dinner party. For up to twelve guests, I prepare three or four kinds of soup, adding another soup for every three to four additional guests. The rest of the menu is simple—some fresh vegetables and dips to nibble as everyone gathers and for serving with the soup, several loaves of freshly baked bread and an assortment of cheeses. For dessert, I serve home-baked pies and cakes.

In this chapter there are also several soups to go into a heated thermos to enjoy at a picnic, on a trek in the woods, or while tailgating before the big game.

WISCONSIN CHEESE CHOWDER

MAKES 4 SERVINGS

There are more than 160 cheese factories in Wisconsin, many of which make a sharp Cheddar cheese that's perfect for this rich soup. The soup needs to be served shortly after it's made, but you can make it ahead of time up to the point of whisking in the cheese. Once the cheese goes in, it'll take only five minutes or so to finish the soup. Traditionally this soup is served with a crisp bacon garnish. I also like to offer a bowl of minced red bell pepper to sprinkle over the soup. The flavor contrast of the sweet pepper and the tart cheese is terrific.

¼ cup (½ stick) butter
1 medium carrot, peeled and finely chopped (¾ cup)
1 medium celery rib, finely chopped (½ cup)
1 small yellow onion, finely chopped (½ cup)
⅓ cup unbleached all-purpose flour
⅛ teaspoon dry mustard
5 cups chicken stock (page 12) or canned low-sodium broth

2 cups shredded sharp yellow Cheddar cheese (½ pound)
Salt, optional, and freshly ground black pepper to taste
4 slices bacon, crisply cooked, drained, and crumbled for garnish, optional
1 small red bell pepper, seeded and finely chopped (½ cup) for garnish, optional

PREP TIME: 20 MIN
COOK TIME: 35 MIN

1. In a 3-quart saucepan, melt butter over medium heat. Add carrot, celery, and onion and sauté until onion is soft but not browned, about 5 minutes. Sprinkle with flour and mustard and cook, stirring frequently, for 5 minutes.

2. Gradually add stock and cook, stirring constantly, until mixture is smooth and bubbly, about 5 minutes. Reduce heat and simmer, uncovered, stirring often, until vegetables are tender, about 15 minutes.

3. Gradually stir in cheese. Simmer over low heat, stirring frequently, until cheese is melted, about 5 minutes. Do not let soup boil. Taste and add salt, if desired, and pepper.

4. To serve, ladle into wide, shallow soup bowls and garnish each serving with bacon and bell pepper. Makes about four 1 ½-cup servings.

1 serving: 443 calories, 18 g protein, 34 g total fat (20.3 g saturated), 17 g carbohydrates, 648 mg sodium, 96 mg cholesterol, 2 g dietary fiber

WHITEFISH CHOWDER

MAKES 6 SERVINGS

Whitefish is a freshwater fish found in the cold waters of the Great Lakes and Hudson Bay. Available both fresh and frozen year-round throughout the Midwest, its mild-flavored, snow-white meat makes a comforting chowder to off-set the effects of a chilly day. Complement this robust soup with plenty of crusty bread and a simple fruit dessert such as baked apples or pears for a satisfying meal. If your market doesn't carry whitefish, you can use other mild-flavored fish such as sea bass, rockfish, sole, or halibut.

1 tablespoon olive oil
1 medium yellow onion, finely chopped
   (1 cup)
1 large garlic clove, minced
1 small fennel bulb, trimmed and
   thinly sliced (1½ cups)
1 medium carrot, peeled and coarsely
   shredded (¾ cup)
1 14½-ounce can plum tomatoes, undrained
   and coarsely chopped
1 sprig fresh thyme or ¼ teaspoon dried,
   crumbled

   Salt, optional, and freshly ground black
   pepper to taste
6 cups chicken stock (page 12) or
   canned low-sodium broth
2 cups water
¾ cup long-grain white rice
1 pound skinless fresh or frozen
   whitefish fillets
¼ teaspoon crushed red pepper flakes
   or to taste
1 pound red-skinned potatoes, quartered
2 tablespoons chopped fresh flat-leaf parsley

1. In a 4-quart soup pot, heat oil over low heat. Add onion and garlic and sauté until onion is soft, about 5 minutes. Add fennel, carrot, and tomatoes with their juice and sauté for 5 minutes. Add thyme and season with salt, if desired, and pepper.

**PREP TIME:
20 MIN
COOK TIME:
35 MIN**

2. Stir in stock, water, and rice. Bring to a boil over medium-high heat. Reduce heat and simmer, uncovered, for 15 minutes. Add fish and simmer until rice is tender and fish flakes easily with a fork, about 5 to 8 minutes. Stir in crushed red pepper.
3. Meanwhile, boil potatoes in water to cover until tender, about 10 minutes. Drain well and toss with parsley.
4. To serve, divide potatoes among 4 wide, shallow soup bowls and ladle in hot soup. Makes about six 2 ½-cup servings.

**1 serving: 319 calories, 19 g protein, 7 g total fat (1.1 g saturated),
44 g carbohydrates, 220 mg sodium, 47 mg cholesterol, 4 g dietary fiber**

GREAT LAKES FISH CHOWDER

MAKES 4 SERVINGS

The lakes and streams of the Heartland are rich with freshwater fish that sustained the early settlers and today provides a bountiful supply to both the commercial and sport fisherman. This is particularly true of the cold lakes in the northern Heartland—the Great Lakes. This recipe calls for curry powder, a spice not uncommon in the Midwest. I first became enamored with curry powder while attending Kansas State University, where we had a large number of students from India, studying home economics and agriculture. The curry adds a gentle warmth to this soup. Serve the chowder for a family supper or an informal dinner with friends, accompanied by a green salad and crisp breadsticks.

2 tablespoons butter
1 large yellow onion, finely chopped (1½ cups)
1 medium leek, white part only, well rinsed and finely chopped (½ cup)
1 medium celery rib with leaves, chopped (¾ cup)
1 large garlic clove, minced
1½ tablespoons curry powder, or to taste
6 cups chicken stock (page 12) or canned low-sodium broth
2 medium thin-skinned potatoes, scrubbed and cut into ½-inch cubes (2 cups)
1 teaspoon chopped fresh oregano leaves or ¼ teaspoon dried, crumbled

1 teaspoon chopped fresh thyme leaves or ¼ teaspoon dried, crumbled
   Salt, optional, and freshly ground black pepper to taste
1 pound fresh or frozen boneless, skinless lake trout, perch, or walleye pike, cut into ½-inch pieces

CONDIMENTS

3 slices bacon, crisply cooked, drained, and crumbled
2 green onions, white part and 1 inch green tops, thinly sliced (¼ cup)
½ cup plain low-fat yogurt
   Hot pepper sauce to taste

PREP TIME: 20 MIN
COOK TIME: 45 MIN

1. In a 4-quart or larger soup pot, melt butter over medium heat. Add onion, leek, celery, and garlic and sauté until onion is soft, about 5 minutes. Add curry powder and cook, stirring occasionally, for 5 minutes.

2. Stir in stock, potatoes, oregano, and thyme. Bring to a boil over medium-high heat. Reduce heat, cover, and simmer until potatoes are tender, about 15 minutes. Taste and add salt, if desired, and pepper.

3. Add fish, cover, and simmer until fish is tender, 5 to 10 minutes.

4. To serve, ladle soup into a heated soup tureen or individual soup bowls. Place bacon, green onions, and yogurt in separate bowls and pass at the table along with hot pepper sauce. Makes about four 2½-cup servings.

1 serving: 322 calories, 28 g protein, 10 g total fat (4.9 g saturated), 30 g carbohydrates, 300 mg sodium, 66 mg cholesterol, 4 g dietary fiber

SALMON CHOWDER

Fishermen in my family have always gone on yearly expeditions to the icy coastal waters of Washington state and sometimes the rivers of Alaska to fish for salmon. But since 1966, the prized coho or silver salmon can also be caught by sports fishermen in the Great Lakes of the Heartland. This firm-textured, pink salmon makes a delicious soup.

1 tablespoon butter

1 medium yellow onion, thinly sliced (1 ½ cups)

1 medium celery rib with leaves, thinly sliced (¾ cup)

1 small carrot, peeled and thinly sliced (½ cup)

3 cups chicken stock (page 12) or canned low-sodium broth

3 small red-skinned potatoes, scrubbed and thinly sliced (1 ½ cups)

1 pound skinless, boneless, salmon fillets, cut into 8 pieces

1 cup half-and-half

4 teaspoons chopped fresh tarragon for garnish, optional

2 slices bacon, crisply cooked, drained, and crumbled for garnish, optional

PREP TIME: 20 MIN

COOK TIME: 35 MIN

1. In a 3-quart saucepan, melt butter over medium heat. Add onion, celery, and carrot and sauté until vegetables are just tender, about 10 minutes.

2. Add stock and potatoes and bring to a boil over medium-high heat. Reduce heat and add salmon pieces. Cover and simmer for 10 to 15 minutes, until potatoes are tender and salmon flakes easily with a fork.

3. Stir in half-and-half until well blended. Heat until soup is steaming but not boiling.

4. To serve, ladle into soup bowls and garnish each serving with a sprinkling of tarragon and bacon. Makes about four 2½-cup servings.

1 serving: 361 calories, 28 g protein, 18 g total fat (8.1 g saturated), 21 g carbohydrates, 215 mg sodium, 81 mg cholesterol, 2 g dietary fiber

FARMERS' MARKET SOUP

MAKES 8 SERVINGS

All over the Heartland during the growing season Saturday is market day, when farmers and amateur gardeners bring their produce still warm from the fields to sell at a farmers' market. Wherever you shop, select the ingredients for this soup according to what's available and what looks good.

¾ cup dried beans (look for unusual ones such as pea beans, white kidney beans, cranberry beans, soy beans, and yellow-eyes), sorted and rinsed

1 ½ pounds ripe tomatoes, red or yellow varieties

1 ½ tablespoons olive oil

1 medium yellow onion, chopped (1 cup)

1 large garlic clove, minced

6 cups chicken stock (page 12) or canned low-sodium broth

1 medium eggplant, deep purple, white, or violet and striated, peeled and chopped (2 cups)

2 medium summer squash, chayote, pattypan, yellow, or zucchini, chopped (2 cups)

1 medium bell pepper, yellow, red, orange, or green, seeded and chopped (1 cup)

½ pound fresh cauliflower florets, coarsely chopped (1 cup)

2 tablespoons slivered fresh basil leaves or 2 teaspoons dried, crumbled

1 teaspoon chopped fresh thyme leaves or ¼ teaspoon dried, crumbled
Salt, optional, and freshly ground black pepper to taste
Garlic Croutons, page 47

PREP TIME: 25 MIN + AT LEAST 1 1/4 HR TO SOAK BEANS
COOK TIME: 1 1/4 HR

1. Put beans in a 6-quart soup pot and cover with 2 inches of water. Soak overnight or for at least 6 hours. Or, bring to a boil over medium-high heat. Remove pan from heat. Cover and let stand for 1 hour. Drain beans and set aside.

2. Meanwhile, score tomatoes on top and bottom. Blanch in boiling water for 30 seconds, then immediately immerse in ice water. Peel the tomatoes and coarsely chop. Set aside.

3. In a 6-quart soup pot, heat oil over medium heat. Add onion, garlic, drained beans, and stock and bring to a boil over medium-high heat. Reduce heat, cover, and simmer, for about 1 hour, until beans are just tender.

4. Add eggplant, squash, bell pepper, cauliflower, herbs, and reserved tomatoes. Taste and season with salt, if desired, and pepper. Bring to a boil over medium-high heat. Reduce heat, cover, and simmer for 10 to 15 minutes, until vegetables are tender.

5. To serve, ladle soup into wide, shallow soup bowls and top each serving with Garlic Croutons. Makes about eight 2-cup servings.

1 serving: 221 calories, 8 g protein, 8 g total fat (3.3 g saturated), 32 g carbohydrates, 186 mg sodium, 12 mg cholesterol, 7 g dietary fiber

GARLIC CROUTONS

MAKES 1 ½ CUPS

¼ pound day-old French bread
   (about 6 slices)
3 tablespoons butter

1 large garlic clove, minced
1 tablespoon chopped fresh
   flat-leaf parsley

Cut bread into ½-inch cubes (you should have about 1½ cups). In a large, heavy skillet, melt butter over medium heat. Add garlic and sauté for 30 seconds. Add bread cubes and sauté until evenly browned, about 10 minutes. Remove pan from heat and toss bread cubes with parsley.

3 tablespoons: 75 calories, 1 g protein, 5 g total fat (2.7 g saturated), 7 g carbohydrates, 124 mg sodium, 11 mg cholesterol, trace dietary fiber

PHEASANT SOUP

MAKES 6 SERVINGS

Wild pheasants are plentiful on my family's Kansas wheat farms, particularly on those in the extreme western regions of the state. Smaller than farm-raised pheasants, they weigh about 1 ½ pounds each and have a gamy but not over-powering flavor. If wild pheasants aren't available, substitute farm-raised pheasants or other game birds such as quail or squab. This elegant clear soup would make a lovely light summer meal that looks, smells, and tastes terrific.

2 whole pheasants (1 ½ pounds each)
2 medium carrots, peeled and cut into large chunks
2 medium yellow onions, peeled and cut in half
2 medium celery ribs, coarsely chopped (1 cup)
2 large garlic cloves, halved
2 ½ quarts chicken stock (page 12) or canned low-sodium broth
2 sprigs fresh thyme or ½ teaspoon dried, crumbled
2 sprigs fresh flat-leaf parsley

1 large bay leaf
6 shiitake mushrooms, cleaned, stems removed, and caps cut into fine julienne strips
¼ pound snow peas, trimmed and cut into fine julienne strips
1 medium carrot, peeled and cut into fine julienne strips
2-inch piece fresh ginger, peeled and cut into fine julienne strips
Snow peas, sliced diagonally for garnish, optional
Carrot curls for garnish, optional

**PREP TIME:
30 MIN
COOK TIME:
1 1/4 HR**

1. Rinse pheasants and pat dry. Discard neck and giblets or reserve for another use. Cut pheasants into quarters.

2. In 6-quart soup pot, combine pheasant pieces, carrot chunks, onions, celery, garlic, and stock. Bring to a boil over medium-high heat. Skim and discard any foam that rises to the top. Add thyme, parsley, and bay leaf. Reduce heat, cover, and simmer until pheasant is tender, about 1 hour, skimming occasionally to keep the broth clear.

3. Using tongs, transfer pheasant pieces to a plate. When cool enough to handle, remove and discard skin and bones. Finely shred the pheasant meat and set aside.

4. Strain the broth through a fine sieve and discard the solids. Return the strained broth to the pot and add the mushrooms, snow peas, julienne carrot, and ginger. Simmer, uncovered, for 5 minutes. Add reserved pheasant meat and simmer for 5 minutes more, until pheasant meat is heated through.

5. To serve, ladle into wide, shallow soup bowls. Garnish each serving with snow pea slices and carrot curls. Makes about six 3-cup servings.

1 serving: 313 calories, 40 g protein, 11 g total fat (3.4 g saturated), 11 g carbohydrates, 148 mg sodium, 117 mg cholesterol, 1 g dietary fiber

CHICKEN SPAETZLE SOUP

MAKES 6 SERVINGS

Literally translated, spaetzle means "little sparrow" in German. The tiny noodles are made from a soft dough of flour and eggs and cooked in simmering water or broth. Frequently served as a separate side dish like potatoes or rice, the spaetzle adds a delightful texture and flavor to this sturdy soup.

SPAETZLE

- 4 large eggs
- ½ cup water
- 1 teaspoon salt
- ¼ teaspoon ground nutmeg
- 2 cups unbleached all-purpose flour
- 1 tablespoon cornstarch
- 1½ tablespoons mild vegetable oil, such as canola

SOUP

- 1 tablespoon olive oil
- 2 medium leeks, white part and 1 inch green, well rinsed and cut into 1-inch rings (1½ cups)
- 2 pounds boneless, skinless chicken breasts
- 2 large carrots, peeled and chopped (2 cups)
- 2 medium celery ribs with leaves, chopped (1 cup)
- 3 sprigs fresh thyme or ½ teaspoon dried, crumbled
- 1 sprig fresh savory or pinch dried, crumbled
- 2 quarts chicken stock (page 12) or canned low-sodium broth
- ½ fresh cauliflower, cored and cut into florets (2 cups)
- 2 medium zucchini, halved lengthwise and cut into 1-inch slices (3 cups)
  Salt, optional, and freshly ground black pepper to taste

PREP TIME: 25 MIN + 1 HOUR FOR SPAETZLE DOUGH TO REST

COOK TIME: 1 HR

1. **To make spaetzle:** In a medium bowl, whisk eggs until frothy. Whisk in water, salt, and nutmeg. Gradually stir in flour and cornstarch until mixture forms a soft dough. Let dough rest for 1 hour. Bring a 4-quart pot of water to a boil. Add 1 tablespoon oil. Place a large colander or all-purpose strainer over boiling water. Place dough in colander and, using the back of a large spoon, press down lightly on the dough to push it through the colander holes into the boiling water. The dough will become easier to force through the colander as it warms over the simmering water. Boil the spaetzle, for about 2 minutes, until it rises to the surface. Using a slotted spoon, remove spaetzle to a bowl of cold water to stop the cooking. Drain well. Gently toss cooked spaetzle with remaining ½ tablespoon oil to coat.

2. **To make soup:** In a 6-quart or larger soup pot, heat the oil over medium heat. Add the leeks and sauté until soft, about 5 minutes.

3. Meanwhile, rinse chicken breasts and pat dry. Remove all visible fat. Cut crosswise into ½-inch-wide strips. Add to pot and cook, stirring occasionally, for 5 minutes. Add carrots, celery, thyme, savory, and stock. Bring to a boil over medium-high heat. Reduce heat, cover, and simmer until chicken is tender, about 20 to 25 minutes.

4. Add cauliflower and simmer, uncovered, for 15 minutes. Add zucchini and simmer for 5 minutes more. Taste and add salt, if desired, and pepper.

5. To serve, add spaetzle to hot soup and ladle into wide, shallow soup bowls. Makes about six 2½-cup servings.

1 serving: 488 calories, 46 g protein, 12 g total fat (2.2 g saturated), 48 g carbohydrates, 601 mg sodium, 229 mg cholesterol, 4 g dietary fiber

TURKEY MINESTRONE

MAKES 6 SERVINGS

A home-style soup that's sure to please the family after the holidays, when there are scraps of turkey left. If you don't have leftover turkey, you can also use cooked chicken.

4   slices bacon, cut into 1-inch pieces
2   medium yellow onions, finely chopped (2 cups)
1   large garlic clove, minced
2   quarts chicken stock (page 12) or canned low-sodium broth
1   14½-ounce can whole tomatoes, undrained and chopped
2   medium thin-skinned potatoes, peeled and diced (2 cups)
1   tablespoon chopped fresh basil leaves or 1 teaspoon dried, crumbled

1   bay leaf
½   cup small shells or elbow macaroni
2   medium zucchini, sliced (3 cups)
1   15-ounce can cannellini beans, drained and rinsed
3   cups chopped cooked turkey meat
    Salt, optional, and freshly ground black pepper to taste
    Freshly grated Parmesan cheese for garnish, optional

**PREP TIME:
20 MIN
COOK TIME:
1 1/4 HR**

1. In a large skillet, cook bacon pieces over medium heat until lightly browned. Using a slotted spoon, remove from skillet and set aside. Add onions and garlic to skillet and sauté until onion is soft, about 5 minutes. Transfer onion, garlic, and bacon to a 6-quart or larger soup pot.

2. Add stock, tomatoes with their juice, potatoes, basil, and bay leaf to the pot. Bring to a boil over medium-high heat. Reduce the heat, cover, and simmer for 30 minutes. Add macaroni and zucchini. Cover and simmer for 10 minutes. Add beans and turkey. Cover and simmer for 10 minutes more. Taste and add salt, if desired, and pepper.

3. To serve, ladle into soup bowls and offer Parmesan cheese to sprinkle over each serving. Makes about six 2 ¾-cup servings.

1 serving: 376 calories, 28 g protein, 13 g total fat (4.5 g saturated), 36 g carbohydrates, 441 mg sodium, 63 mg cholesterol, 5 g dietary fiber

AUTUMN RABBIT SOUP

MAKES 4 SERVINGS

Rabbit is quite popular in the northern regions of the Heartland, particularly in Minnesota and Wisconsin, where vast numbers of Eastern Europeans settled. The first time I ate rabbit I was surprised by its leanness and depth of flavor—similar to, but richer than, chicken. Frozen rabbit is available in most supermarkets. Thaw it in the refrigerator overnight. This soup can also be made with chicken; remove the chicken skin after cooking.

⅓ cup wild rice, well rinsed
1 cup water
2 tablespoons butter
2 medium yellow onions, quartered and thinly sliced (3 cups)
1 large red bell pepper, seeded and chopped (1½ cups)
2 medium celery ribs, thinly sliced (1 cup)
1 medium carrot, peeled and thinly sliced (¾ cup)
1 rabbit (2¾ to 3 pounds), cut into 8 pieces

Salt, optional, and freshly ground black pepper to taste
1 14½-ounce can plum tomatoes, undrained
6 cups chicken stock (page 12) or canned low-sodium broth
2 tablespoons chopped fresh flat-leaf parsley
2 teaspoons Worcestershire sauce
2 tablespoons chopped fresh chervil or parsley for garnish, optional
Finely chopped red onion for garnish, optional

PREP TIME: 20 MIN
COOK TIME: 50 MIN

1. In a small saucepan, bring wild rice and water to a boil. Reduce heat, cover, and simmer until rice is just tender, about 45 minutes. Drain if necessary.

2. Meanwhile, in a 4-quart or larger soup pot, melt butter over medium heat. Add onions, bell pepper, celery, and carrot and sauté until onions are soft but not browned, about 5 minutes.

3. Rinse rabbit pieces and pat dry. Season with salt, if desired, and pepper. Add rabbit pieces, tomatoes with their juice, stock, parsley, and Worcestershire sauce to pot. Bring to a boil over medium-high heat. Reduce heat, partially cover, and simmer until rabbit is cooked through, about 30 minutes.

4. Using tongs, transfer rabbit pieces to a plate and cool slightly. Cut rabbit meat away from the bones and finely shred. Return meat to pot. Stir in rice. Simmer for 5 minutes.

5. To serve, ladle into soup bowls and garnish each serving with a sprinkling of fresh chervil and chopped red onion. Makes about four 3-cup servings.

1 serving: 552 calories, 57 g protein, 21 g total fat (8.0 g saturated), 32 g carbohydrates, 446 mg sodium, 163 mg cholesterol, 5 g dietary fiber

LENTIL SOUP

MAKES 8 SERVINGS

When I was growing up in Kansas, I don't think I even knew what a lentil was. It wasn't until years later that I became fond of them in soups, salads, and casseroles. Nowadays, most Heartland roadside diners and cafes feature lentil soup during the winter months to ward off the chill. This soup is so hearty that I use the sausage sparingly.

2 tablespoons olive oil	2½ cups dried lentils, sorted and rinsed
2 medium celery ribs, chopped (1 cup)	1 14½-ounce can whole tomatoes, undrained
1 medium yellow onion, finely chopped (1 cup)	1 tablespoon chopped fresh thyme leaves or 1 teaspoon dried, crumbled
1 medium red bell pepper, seeded and chopped (1 cup)	1½ teaspoons chopped fresh oregano leaves or ½ teaspoon dried, crumbled
1 medium carrot, peeled and chopped (¾ cup)	1 bay leaf
2 large garlic cloves, minced	Salt, optional, and freshly ground black pepper to taste
2 quarts chicken stock (page 12) or canned low-sodium broth	¼ pound smoked fully cooked sausage such as kielbasa
½ cup red wine or additional stock	Chopped fresh parsley for garnish, optional

PREP TIME: 20 MIN

COOK TIME: 55 MIN

1. In a 6-quart soup pot, heat oil over medium heat. Add celery, onion, bell pepper, carrot, and garlic and sauté until onion is soft, about 5 minutes.

2. Add stock, wine, lentils, tomatoes with their juice, thyme, oregano, and bay leaf. Bring to a boil over medium-high heat. Reduce heat and simmer, partially covered, for 35 to 45 minutes, until lentils are tender. Discard bay leaf.

3. In a food processor or blender, puree 1 cup of soup. Stir the puree into the soup. Taste and add salt, if desired, and pepper.

4. To serve, cut sausage into thin slivers. Ladle soup into wide, shallow soup bowls and sprinkle each serving with sausage. Makes about eight 2½-cup servings.

1 serving: 329 calories, 20 g protein, 8 g total fat (2.0 g saturated), 44 g carbohydrates, 306 mg sodium, 10 mg cholesterol, 9 g dietary fiber

GARDEN BEEF SOUP

MAKES 6 SERVINGS

This is the kind of home-style soup that's been simmering on the stoves of Heartlanders since the settlers planted their first vegetable garden. Cinnamon was often used by early farm wives in meat and poultry dishes; it adds a subtle flavor to this soup.

3 tablespoons unbleached all-purpose flour
1 teaspoon ground cinnamon
1 teaspoon fresh thyme leaves
   or ¼ teaspoon dried, crumbled
½ teaspoon salt, optional
½ teaspoon freshly ground black pepper
1¼ pounds beef tenderloin or sirloin tips,
   cut into 1-inch pieces
2 tablespoons olive oil
1 medium yellow onion, quartered and
   thinly sliced (1 ½ cups)

1 large garlic clove, minced
3 small russet potatoes, peeled and
   diced (1 ½ cups)
2 medium carrots, peeled and thinly
   sliced (1 ½ cups)
2 medium celery ribs, thinly sliced (1 cup)
2 quarts beef stock (page 13) or canned
   low-sodium broth
1 cup fresh or frozen peas
½ cup chopped celery leaves for garnish,
   optional

PREP TIME: 20 MIN
COOK TIME: 1 1/4 HR

1. In a large zipper-type plastic bag, mix flour, cinnamon, thyme, salt, if desired, and pepper. Add beef, seal bag, and shake to coat evenly.

2. In a 4-quart or larger soup pot, heat oil over medium heat. Add seasoned beef pieces and brown on all sides, about 5 minutes. Add onion and garlic and cook, stirring frequently, for 5 minutes. Add potatoes, carrots, celery, and stock. Bring to a boil over medium-high heat. Reduce heat, cover, and simmer until beef and vegetables are tender when pierced with a fork, about 1 hour.

3. Add peas, cover, and simmer until peas are tender, about 5 to 10 minutes more.

4. To serve, ladle into soup bowls and garnish each serving with celery leaves. Makes about six 2 ½-cup servings.

1 serving: 304 calories, 26 g protein, 13 g total fat (3.6 g saturated), 20 g carbohydrates, 305 mg sodium, 59 mg cholesterol, 4 g dietary fiber

GOULASH SOUP

My mother used to make a terrific goulash when I was growing up in Kansas. Mildly spicy with lots of poppy-red paprika, it was one of my favorite meals. Thinned a bit, it makes a marvelous soup to serve with crusty black bread and a crock of sweet butter.

4 slices lean bacon, cut into 1-inch pieces	1 large green bell pepper, seeded and cut into 1-inch pieces (1 ½ cups)
1 large yellow onion, chopped (1 ½ cups)	2 medium thin-skinned potatoes, peeled and cut into ½-inch cubes (2 cups)
2 large garlic cloves, minced	2 large plum tomatoes, chopped (1 cup)
2 tablespoons hot paprika, or to taste	¼ pound dried wide egg noodles
1 teaspoon caraway seeds	Salt, optional, and freshly ground black pepper to taste
2 pounds boneless beef chuck, cut into 1-inch cubes	Chopped fresh parsley for garnish, optional
2 quarts beef stock (page 13) or canned low-sodium broth	

PREP TIME: 20 MIN
COOK TIME: 2 3/4 HR

1. In a 6-quart or larger soup pot, cook bacon over medium heat until crisp. Using a slotted spoon, transfer to paper towels to drain. Set aside.

2. Remove and discard all but 1 tablespoon of the bacon drippings. Add onion and garlic to reserved drippings and sauté over medium heat until onion is soft, about 5 minutes. Stir in paprika and caraway seeds. Add beef, stock, and bell pepper. Bring to a boil over medium-high heat. Reduce heat, cover, and simmer until meat is tender when pierced, about 2 hours.

3. Add potatoes and tomatoes. Cover and simmer for 10 minutes. Stir in noodles and simmer until noodles and potatoes are tender, about 10 minutes. Taste and add salt, if desired, and pepper.

4. To serve, ladle into wide, shallow soup bowls and garnish each serving with chopped parsley and reserved bacon. Makes about six 2 ½-cup servings.

1 serving: 440 calories, 43 g protein, 15 g total fat (5.4 g saturated), 31 g carbohydrates, 207 mg sodium, 128 mg cholesterol, 3 g dietary fiber

HAM AND SWEET POTATO CHOWDER

MAKES 4 SERVINGS

If you're purchasing a bone-in country ham for Sunday dinner, have the butcher saw off the hock to use in this soup. Otherwise, buy a ham hock or 1 ½ pounds bone-in smoked pork chops. This would be a terrific soup to take in a preheated thermos for a winter outing.

1 tablespoon olive oil
2 medium red bell peppers, seeded and chopped (2 cups)
1 large yellow onion, chopped (1 ½ cups)
1 large garlic clove, minced
1 smoked ham hock (about 1 ½ pounds)
3 medium sweet potatoes, peeled and cut into 1-inch pieces (4 cups)

6 sprigs fresh thyme or 1 teaspoon dried, crumbled
1 large bay leaf
1 teaspoon ground cumin
⅛ teaspoon ground cinnamon
⅛ teaspoon ground nutmeg
6 cups chicken stock (page 12) or canned low-sodium broth
1 cup half-and-half

PREP TIME: 20 MIN
COOK TIME: 1 HR

1. In a 4-quart or larger soup pot, heat oil over medium-high heat. Add bell peppers and sauté until soft, about 5 minutes. Add onion and garlic and sauté until onion is soft, about 5 minutes.

2. Add ham hock, sweet potatoes, thyme, bay leaf, cumin, cinnamon, nutmeg, and stock. Bring to a boil over medium-high heat, stirring to keep vegetables from sticking. Reduce heat, cover, and simmer for 45 minutes, until potatoes are tender.

3. Using a slotted spoon, remove ham hock and set aside to cool. Discard thyme sprigs and bay leaf. Remove meat from ham hocks and cut into ¼-inch-thick strips. Set aside.

4. In a food processor or blender, puree soup in batches. Return soup to pot and stir in half-and-half until well blended. Cook, uncovered, over medium heat, stirring constantly, until soup is steaming but not boiling.

5. To serve, ladle into soup bowls and scatter ham over each serving. Makes about four 3-cup servings.

1 serving: 475 calories, 21 g protein, 24 g total fat (9.7 g saturated), 44 g carbohydrates, 293 mg sodium, 84 mg cholesterol, 5 g dietary fiber

PORK AND BEAN SOUP

MAKES 4 SERVINGS

This soup gets a jump start with canned pork and beans, a nostalgic part of most everyone's childhood, especially for those of us who grew up in the Midwest. Fortified with garlic-flavored sausage or Polish kielbasa, the soup goes together quickly and is sure to be a hit with the youngest to the oldest members of your family. This recipe can also be made using turkey sausage and reduced-fat pork and beans.

1 tablespoon olive oil
1 medium yellow onion, finely chopped
   (1 cup)
1 large garlic clove, minced
1 medium green bell pepper, seeded and
   finely chopped (1 cup)
1 medium carrot, peeled and thinly sliced
   (¾ cup)

1 pound garlic-flavored sausage or Polish
   kielbasa, cut into 1-inch-thick slices
1 medium tomato, chopped (1 cup)
5 cups beef stock (page 13) or
   low-sodium canned broth
2 15 ½-ounce cans pork and beans, undrained
¼ teaspoon dry mustard
   Freshly ground black pepper to taste
   Sour cream for garnish, optional

**PREP TIME:
15 MIN
COOK TIME:
40 MIN**

1. In a 4-quart soup pot, heat oil over medium heat. Add onion and garlic and sauté until onion is soft, about 5 minutes. Add bell pepper, carrot, and sausage and sauté until vegetables begin to soften, about 10 minutes.

2. Add tomato and stock and bring to a boil over medium-high heat. Reduce heat, cover, and simmer for 10 minutes. Stir in pork and beans and mustard. Cover and simmer for 10 minutes more. Taste and add pepper.

3. To serve, ladle into soup bowls and garnish each serving with a dollop of sour cream. Makes about four 3-cup servings.

1 serving: 615 calories, 29 g protein, 38 g total fat (12.0 g saturated), 52 g carbohydrates, 1,976 mg sodium, 76 mg cholesterol, 12 g dietary fiber

SHRIMP AND TOMATO SOUP

MAKES 4 SERVINGS

If you have tomatoes ripening in the garden when you make this soup, by all means use them. Serve with warm baking powder biscuits or mini corn muffins.

1 tablespoon olive oil
1 small yellow onion, finely chopped (½ cup)
1 small celery rib, finely chopped (¼ cup)
1 large garlic clove, minced
1 quart chicken stock (page 12) or canned low-sodium broth
1 14 ½-ounce can whole tomatoes, undrained

1 medium thin-skinned potato, peeled and cut into thin julienne strips (1 cup)
½ teaspoon dried Italian herb seasoning, crumbled
½ pound small peeled, deveined cooked shrimp
Salt, optional, and freshly ground black pepper to taste
Chopped fresh parsley for garnish, optional
Hot pepper sauce, optional

PREP TIME: 15 MIN

MICRO-COOK TIME: 23 MIN

1. In a deep 4- or 5-quart microwave-safe casserole or tureen, combine oil, onion, celery, and garlic. Cover with a lid or vented plastic wrap and microwave on HIGH (100 percent power) for 8 minutes, until onion and celery are soft, stirring twice.
2. Stir in stock, tomatoes with their juice, potato strips, and Italian seasoning. Cover and microwave on HIGH for 8 to 10 minutes, until soup is hot, stirring twice. Stir in shrimp and microwave on HIGH for 3 to 5 minutes more, stirring once.
3. To serve, taste and add salt, if desired, and pepper. Ladle into soup bowls and garnish each serving with chopped parsley. Add hot pepper sauce as desired. Makes about four 2½-cup servings.

1 serving: 160 calories, 14 g protein, 4 g total fat (0.7 g saturated), 17 g carbohydrates, 350 mg sodium, 111 mg cholesterol, 2 g dietary fiber

MICROWAVE COOKING TIMES

For testing these recipes, a 650-watt microwave oven was used. Cooking times may vary if you have a more powerful microwave.

VELVET CHICKEN SOUP

MAKES 4 SERVINGS

My mother used to make this soup on the stovetop, but using the microwave cuts down considerably on the cooking time. After the holidays, make the soup with leftover turkey instead of chicken.

¼ cup (½ stick) butter
1 small yellow onion, finely chopped (½ cup)
2 tablespoons unbleached all-purpose flour
3 cups chicken stock (page 12) or canned low-sodium broth

1 cup sour cream
1 ½ cups chopped cooked chicken
  Salt, optional, and freshly ground black pepper to taste

PREP TIME:
5 MIN
MICRO-COOK
TIME:
14 MIN

1. In a 4- or 5-quart microwave-safe casserole or soup tureen, melt butter, uncovered, for 30 seconds on HIGH (100 percent power). Add onion and microwave, uncovered, on HIGH for 5 minutes, stirring twice. Stir in flour and 1 cup stock. Microwave, uncovered, on HIGH for 1 minute.

2. Transfer mixture to a food processor or blender and process until smooth. Return mixture to casserole. Whisk in remaining stock until smooth. Stir in chicken.

3. Cover with a lid or vented plastic wrap and microwave on HIGH until hot, about 5 minutes, stirring twice. Stir in sour cream and microwave on HIGH 2 minutes more, stirring after 1 minute. Do not allow soup to boil.

4. To serve, taste and add salt, if desired, and pepper. Ladle into soup bowls. Makes about four 1 ½-cup servings.

1 serving: 356 calories, 18 g protein, 28 g total fat (15.7 g saturated), 9 g carbohydrates, 228 mg sodium, 103 mg cholesterol, trace dietary fiber

CHILI CLAM CHOWDER

MAKES 4 SERVINGS

Since I've always been fond of spicy foods, I couldn't resist transforming clam chowder into something spicy. I think you'll love the change, too.

1 35-ounce can whole tomatoes, undrained
1 16-ounce can small whole onions, drained
1 16-ounce can small potatoes, drained and halved
1 12-ounce can baby clams, undrained

2 teaspoons chili powder
1 teaspoon chopped fresh oregano leaves or ¼ teaspoon dried, crumbled
¼ teaspoon ground cumin
   Freshly ground black pepper to taste
¼ cup finely chopped fresh cilantro for garnish, optional

PREP TIME: 10 MIN
MICRO-COOK TIME: 15 MIN

1. In a food processor or blender, process tomatoes with their juice until smooth. Pour mixture into a deep 4- or 5-quart microwave-safe casserole or soup tureen.

2. Add onions and potatoes. Drain clams and add their liquid to casserole. Set clams aside. Stir chili powder, oregano, and cumin into soup. Cover with a lid or vented plastic wrap and microwave on HIGH (100 percent power) for 10 to 12 minutes, or until steaming hot, stirring twice.

3. Stir in reserved clams. Cover and microwave on HIGH 2 to 3 minutes more, stirring twice.

4. To serve, taste and add pepper. Ladle into soup bowls and garnish each serving with chopped cilantro. Makes about four 2½-cup servings.

1 serving: 189 calories, 16 g protein, 2 g total fat (0.3 g saturated), 29 g carbohydrates, 1,090 mg sodium, 30 mg cholesterol, 5 g dietary fiber

SPICY SAUSAGE SOUP

I first ate a soup like this at a Mexican restaurant in Indianapolis. It's quite thick, like chili—I prefer it this way, but if you wish, you can thin it down with a little water or tomato juice.

½ pound bulk pork sausage
1 small yellow onion, finely chopped
  (½ cup)
1 large garlic clove, minced
2 15-ounce cans red kidney beans, drained
2 14½-ounce cans stewed tomatoes,
  undrained
2 teaspoons chili powder
1 teaspoon fresh thyme leaves
  or ¼ teaspoon dried, crumbled

½ teaspoon ground cumin
2 tablespoons balsamic vinegar
  Freshly ground black pepper to taste
CONDIMENTS
⅓ cup shredded Cheddar cheese
⅓ cup crushed tortilla chips
¼ cup sour cream
2 green onions, white part with 1 inch
  green tops, thinly sliced (¼ cup)

**PREP TIME:
15 MIN
MICRO-COOK
TIME: 20 MIN**

1. In a deep 4- or 5-quart microwave-safe casserole or tureen, crumble sausage. Cover with a lid or vented plastic wrap and microwave on HIGH (100 percent power) for 5 minutes, stirring twice. Using a slotted spoon, remove sausage to paper towels to drain. Set aside.

2. Add onion and garlic to sausage drippings. Cover and microwave on HIGH for 5 minutes, stirring twice. Drain and discard all fat.

3. Return sausage to casserole and add beans, tomatoes, chili powder, thyme, and cumin. Stir until well blended. Cover and microwave on HIGH until soup is hot, about 10 minutes, stirring 2 or 3 times. Stir in vinegar. Taste and add pepper.

4. To serve, divide Cheddar cheese and crushed tortilla chips among 4 wide, shallow soup bowls. Ladle in hot soup and garnish each serving with a dollop of sour cream and green onions. Makes about four 2-cup servings.

1 serving: 471 calories, 23 g protein, 18 g total fat (7.4 g saturated), 57 g carbohydrates, 1,016 mg sodium, 40 mg cholesterol, 19 g dietary fiber

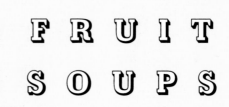

FRUIT SOUPS

FRUIT SOUPS HAVE ALWAYS BEEN popular in the Heartland, particularly among the immigrants from northern Europe — Norway, Sweden, Denmark, Finland, Germany, Poland, and Russia. Fragrant and rich in flavor, fruit soups can be offered as a refreshing beginning of a summer meal, as a delicious cold snack, as a dramatic ending of a special dinner, or as a sweet temptation for breakfast or brunch.

The fruit of the Midwest is extensive — from apples, pears, peaches, and plums grown in almost every state to ten kinds of berries (blackberries, blueberries, cranberries, currants, elderberries, gooseberries, lingonberries, mulberries, raspberries, and strawberries). Michigan grows more than 75 percent of the nation's cherries, and many farmers' markets carry locally grown grapes.

This collection of fruit soups includes both cooked and uncooked versions. Some are thick and chunky; others are smooth and light, perfect for sipping from sugar-rimmed goblets. All of them, such as Rhubarb Buttermilk Soup and Sparkling Cranberry Soup are sensational treats.

RHUBARB BUTTERMILK SOUP

MAKES 4 SERVINGS

Rhubarb is a favorite among Midwestern cooks for pies, crisps, and sauces. The tart fruit (botanically it's actually a vegetable) also makes an excellent soup. A delicate pink color, this refreshing soup uses buttermilk, another Heartland favorite. If you are using frozen rhubarb, make sure it has not been pre-sweetened. This controls the sweetness of the finished soup.

½ pound rhubarb (about 6 stalks), trimmed and rinsed, or 1 ½ cups thawed and drained frozen rhubarb
⅓ cup sugar
¼ cup water
3 tablespoons fresh lemon juice (1 large lemon)

1 teaspoon grated lemon rind
1 cup low-fat (1.5%) buttermilk
1 cup half-and-half
⅛ teaspoon ground allspice
⅛ teaspoon ground cinnamon
2 tablespoons sliced almonds for garnish, optional

PREP TIME:
10 MIN
COOK TIME:
25 MIN
CHILL TIME:
AT LEAST
4 HR

1. Cut rhubarb into 1-inch pieces. In a 3-quart saucepan, combine rhubarb, sugar, water, lemon juice, and lemon rind. Bring to a boil over medium-high heat. Reduce heat, cover, and simmer for 20 minutes, stirring once. Transfer mixture to a nonreactive bowl and let cool. Cover and chill for at least 30 minutes.
2. Stir in buttermilk, half-and-half, allspice, and cinnamon. Cover and chill for at least 3 ½ hours more or overnight.
3. To serve, stir well before ladling into soup bowls. Garnish each serving with a few sliced almonds. Makes about four 1-cup servings.

1 serving: 202 calories, 5 g protein, 9 g total fat (4.9 g saturated), 27 g carbohydrates, 92 mg sodium, 24 mg cholesterol, 1 g dietary fiber

BLUEBERRY-BLACKBERRY SOUP

Michigan is blueberry country, where one's likely to run across patches of tiny wild blueberries growing alongside country roads, as well as vast farms of cultivated berries. Teamed with blackberries, they make a vivid soup that can also be prepared with raspberries, loganberries, or strawberries. If fresh berries aren't in season, you can substitute unsweetened frozen whole berries, thawed and well drained.

1 ½ cups fresh or frozen unsweetened
blueberries
1 ½ cups fresh or frozen unsweetened
blackberries
2 cups water
3 tablespoons quick-cooking tapioca

½ to ¾ cup sugar
1 ½ tablespoons fresh lemon juice
1 teaspoon grated lemon rind
⅓ cup sour cream
Ground cinnamon for garnish,
optional

PREP TIME:
15 MIN
COOK TIME:
10 MIN
CHILL TIME:
AT LEAST
4 HR

1. Rinse and pick over berries. Drain well. Set aside.

2. In a 3-quart saucepan over medium-high heat, mix water, tapioca, ½ cup sugar, lemon juice, and grated lemon rind. Bring to a boil over medium-high heat, stirring constantly. Reduce heat and add berries. Simmer, stirring constantly, for 5 minutes. Remove from heat. Taste and stir in remaining ¼ cup sugar, if desired.

3. In a food processor or blender, puree soup in batches. Strain through a sieve lined with cheesecloth to remove any seeds. Transfer soup to a nonreactive bowl and let cool. Cover and chill for at least 4 hours or overnight.

4. To serve, stir well before ladling into soup bowls. Garnish each serving with dollop of sour cream and a sprinkling of cinnamon. Makes about six ¾-cup servings.

1 serving: 148 calories, 1 g protein, 3 g total fat (1.7 g saturated), 32 g carbohydrates, 9 mg sodium, 6 mg cholesterol, 3 g dietary fiber

CHERRY SOUP

MAKES 6 SERVINGS

This recipe comes from Jane Baker, marketing director of the Cherry Marketing Institute of Oke-mos, Michigan. Tart cherries, sometimes called pie cherries, are rarely sold fresh because they are highly perishable. Harvested, pitted, and processed within twenty-four hours, they are full of fresh cherry flavor. Frozen tart cherries are available at most supermarkets. Look for dried tart cherries at specialty food shops and some large supermarkets. They are also available by mail order (see Sources, page 142). If you like, add a splash of kirsch to each serving.

½ cup frozen unsweetened tart cherries, thawed	1 tablespoon grenadine
½ cup frozen dark sweet cherries, thawed	1 tablespoon sugar or to taste
1 cup custard-style cherry yogurt	¼ teaspoon ground nutmeg
1 cup sour cream	Kirsch (cherry brandy), optional
1 cup heavy cream	Grated orange rind for garnish, optional
½ cup dried tart cherries	Sprigs fresh mint for garnish, optional

**PREP TIME:
10 MIN

CHILL TIME:
AT LEAST
4 HR**

1. In a food processor or blender, puree thawed tart and sweet cherries with juices. Set aside.

2. In a large bowl, mix yogurt, sour cream, heavy cream, and dried cherries. Add pureed cherries, grenadine, sugar, and nutmeg and mix well. Cover and chill for at least 4 hours or overnight.

3. To serve, stir well before ladling into soup bowls. Add a splash of kirsch to each serving and garnish with grated orange rind and sprig of mint. Makes about six ½-cup servings.

1 serving: 324 calories, 4 g protein, 23 g total fat (14.4 g saturated), 27 g carbohydrates, 60 mg sodium, 73 mg cholesterol, 1 g dietary fiber

STRAWBERRY MELON SOUP

MAKES 8 SERVINGS

This is a spectacular summer soup, two fruit purees poured into a bowl without mixing. The two-toned soup swirls together in pretty patterns as it's eaten, blending the fresh tastes of the two fruits. This soup can also be made with red raspberries or blackberries instead of the strawberries.

4 cups peeled, seeded, and chopped ripe
   honeydew melon
¼ cup fresh lime juice (2 large limes)
1 ½ tablespoons sugar
2 pints fresh strawberries, rinsed and hulled

½ cup dry red wine or white
   grape juice
⅛ teaspoon cayenne pepper
   Freshly cracked peppercorns for garnish,
   optional

**PREP TIME:
15 MIN
CHILL TIME:
AT LEAST
4 HR**

1. In a food processor or blender, puree melon, lime juice, and sugar. Transfer mixture to a nonreactive bowl. Cover and chill for at least 4 hours or overnight.
2. In a food processor or blender, puree strawberries, wine, and cayenne. Transfer mixture to a nonreactive bowl. Cover and chill chill for at least 4 hours or overnight.
3. To serve, simultaneously ladle (or pour from 2 pitchers) about ½ cup of each soup into opposite sides of wide, shallow soup bowls. (The soups have the same consistency, so they won't blend.) Garnish the honeydew soup with a few freshly cracked peppercorns.

Makes about eight 1-cup servings.

1 serving: 73 calories, 1 g protein, 0 total fat (0 saturated), 16 g carbohydrates, 10 mg sodium, 0 cholesterol, 2 g dietary fiber

PEACH SOUP

Every summer we used to pick several bushels of fresh peaches at U-Pick farms south of Wichita, Kansas. The sweet fruit combines with melon to make a wonderful soup—frothy and refreshing with a dollop of whipped cream—that's appropriate for dessert or a special Sunday brunch. Canned or frozen peaches are not recommended.

6 large ripe peaches (about 3 pounds), peeled, pitted, and sliced
½ medium ripe melon such as cantaloupe or casaba, peeled, seeded, and chopped (2 cups)
⅓ cup fresh orange juice (1 medium orange)

¼ cup dry white wine
3 tablespoons sugar
⅛ teaspoon cayenne pepper
Whipped cream for garnish, optional
Sprigs fresh mint for garnish, optional

PREP TIME: 20 MIN
CHILL TIME: AT LEAST 4 HR

1. In a food processor or blender, puree peaches and melon. With machine running, add orange juice, wine, sugar, and cayenne and process until well blended.
2. Transfer mixture to a nonreactive bowl. Cover and chill for at least 4 hours or overnight.
3. To serve, stir well before ladling into small soup bowls. Spoon whipped cream onto each serving and garnish with a sprig of fresh mint. Makes about six 1-cup servings.

1 serving: 130 calories, 2 g protein, 0 total fat (0 saturated), 31 g carbohydrates, 5 mg sodium, 0 cholesterol, 4 g dietary fiber

SPARKLING CRANBERRY SOUP

MAKES 6 SERVINGS

Every October thousands of Heartland visitors convene in the Eagle River area of Wisconsin for the annual cranberry festival. (Wisconsin vies with Massachusetts as the top producer of fresh cranberries in the nation.) At the festival you can visit working cranberry bogs, sip cranberry wine, buy cranberry candy, and watch the cranberry cook-off. The crème fraîche for this soup takes thirty-six hours to make, so plan ahead.

1 12-ounce bag fresh cranberries,
   sorted and rinsed
3 cups water
¼ cup sugar
1 3-inch cinnamon stick
2 whole cloves

2 tablespoons cornstarch dissolved
   in 3 tablespoons cold water
2 tablespoons fresh lemon juice
1 cup chilled champagne or ginger ale
6 tablespoons crème fraîche (page 25)
   for garnish, optional

**PREP TIME:
10 MIN + 36 HR
TO MAKE
CRÈME FRAÎCHE
(IF USING)
COOK TIME:
40 MIN
CHILL TIME:
AT LEAST
4 HR**

1. In a medium, heavy saucepan, combine cranberries, water, sugar, cinnamon stick, and cloves. Bring to a boil over medium-high heat. Reduce heat, cover, and simmer for 30 minutes.

2. Stir in cornstarch mixture and simmer, stirring constantly, until liquid is clear and thickened. Stir in lemon juice.

3. Transfer soup to a nonreactive bowl and let cool. Tightly cover and chill for at least 4 hours or overnight.

4. To serve, discard cinnamon stick and cloves. Stir in the champagne until well blended and ladle into sugar-rimmed stemmed glasses or small soup bowls. Spoon 1 tablespoon of crème fraîche over each serving. Makes about six 1-cup servings.

1 serving: 143 calories, 1 g protein, 4 g total fat (2.7 g saturated), 20 g carbohydrates, 10 mg sodium, 13 mg cholesterol, 2 g dietary fiber

S A L A D S

SALADS IN THE HEARTLAND ARE more varied than ever. This food category has seen dramatic changes. Not that long ago one could expect most green salads to contain iceberg or romaine lettuce, the primary ingredients for seafood salads to come from a can, and fruit salads to be dictated by season.

In looking through my collection of Heartland community cookbooks from the 1950s, I can detect the promise of change: avocados were beginning to be used in salads, Bermuda onions were considered "best" for salads, bean salads were occasionally molded, and Caesar salad had just emerged in the Midwest. During this time restaurants were also starting to feature salad buffets (a forerunner of today's salad bar) and salad trolleys—a cart filled with a small selection of salads that was rolled up to the table.

When I was growing up in Kansas, a basic salad was usually served with the evening meal. Today the salad of the Heartland cook is anything but predictable. It appears as a light prelude to the meal, as a substantial side dish, as a meal-in-one, or even as a follow-up to dinner. Throughout the Heartland people are returning to home gardening— whether in urban community plots, backyard gardens intermixed with flowers, or serious kitchen gardens of farm wives that look like miniature farms themselves.

The recipes that follow are a contemporary collection of salads to tease and please your senses— salads that are dressed smartly for holidays and special occasions, savory salads based on healthy grains and legumes, refreshing fruit salads, and molded salads that shimmer and sparkle. No longer just tossed together, some of these salads are carefully composed to be as visually attractive as they are delicious to eat. The recipes range from simple to simply extravagant, with each featuring ingredients indigenous to the Heartland.

RINSING AND CRISPING GREENS

Salad greens require careful handling to avoid bruising. Rinse thoroughly in cold water, removing sand or silt (even packaged mixed greens that indicate they're prewashed need a light rinsing at home). Wrap the greens in paper towels and place them in a plastic bag (don't seal it). Store in the crisper unit of your refrigerator until ready to use.

SALAD GREENS

Here are the salad greens you're likely to encounter in today's supermarkets and produce stands, sold separately or mixed together:

Arugula: Elongated, dark green leaves resembling large radish leaves with a peppery taste. Use arugula, also known as rocket, to accent milder greens in salads.

Baby Lettuces: Available in a variety of colors, textures, and flavors, these young lettuces are known for their mild fresh-from-the-garden flavor and delicate, tender leaves. Look for leaves that are not torn or bruised.

Belgian Endive: The mildest member of the chicory family, these spear-shaped heads contain slender creamy white leaves with pale yellow tips. Select heads that are firm and crisp, with tightly furled leaves. The slightly bitter flavor complements mild lettuces.

Butterhead Lettuce (also called **Boston or Bibb**): Small loosely formed heads of lettuce with pale green leaves and a mild, sweet flavor.

Chicory: Also called curly endive, this green has crisp frilly, narrow dark green leaves that curl at the edges. It has a pleasantly bitter taste that is best used in a mixture with other greens.

Frisée: A frizzy version of curly endive with leaves that range in color from ivory to deep chartreuse. Available sporadically year-round, it is usually included in the European-style pre-packaged salad blends.

Leaf Lettuce: This lettuce contains large soft, ruffly leaves that are bright green or green with bronze-red tips. The tender leaves are loosely attached and have a delicate flavor. They are available year-round and easily home grown.

Mâche: Also called corn salad, lamb's lettuce, lamb's tongue, or field salad. This green has bright green violet-shaped leaves with a tangy, nutlike flavor.

Mesclun: A specialty from the region around Nice, in southern France, it is sold by the pound or in prepackaged blends in produce markets and some large supermarket chains. A blend of eight to twelve varieties of baby lettuce leaves, savory herbs, edible petals, and wild greens. Mesclun is easily grown in the home garden; harvesting can start six weeks after sowing the seeds.

Radicchio: A member of the chicory family, the most widely available variety is *radicchio di Verona*, with ruby-red leaves, white ribs and a bitter, peppery bite. The leaves form small compact heads.

Romaine: Large broad lettuce leaves with a crisp texture that branch from a white base. The slightly bitter leaves range in color from dark green outer leaves to pale yellow inner leaves.

Spinach: Long-stemmed, slightly bitter dark green leaves that, depending on the variety, are smooth or curled. It is sold loose or packaged and is available year-round. Baby spinach is also available.

Watercress: A member of the mustard family, this delicate salad green has small crisp dark green leaves and edible stems with a peppery bite. Watercress is available year-round and is usually sold in small bunches.

VEGETABLE AND GREEN SALADS

YOU'LL FIND DOZENS OF INTRIGUING recipes for vegetable and green salads in this chapter. When the summer sizzles with unbearable heat, demanding something light and cool to eat, serve a crisp leafy salad dressed with a fruity vinaigrette to stimulate flagging appetites. As the colors of the land turn from summer green to autumn gold and russet, intensify salad flavors using combinations of crunchy vegetables, nutty-flavored grains, and creamy home-made dressings. And when winter sets in, add spicy ingredients and use warm dressings to keep the cold weather at bay.

With today's hothouses and overnight air-freight delivery, out-of-season fruits and vegetables are now available in markets to supplement native produce. We're experiencing a revolution in the salad bowl.

Whether it's a beautiful green salad to begin or accompany a meal or a vegetable salad to bring to a potluck party or backyard picnic, these dishes will add excitement to almost any menu or gathering.

FRUITED SPINACH SALAD WITH POPPY SEED DRESSING

MAKES 6 SERVINGS

Several fine restaurants and inns in the Heartland serve a crisp spinach salad with strawberries or raspberries and a piquant poppy seed dressing. My version has the crunchy addition of fresh bean sprouts and toasted walnuts. Make the dressing ahead so the flavor has time to develop.

POPPY SEED DRESSING
½ cup sugar
¼ cup white wine vinegar
1 tablespoon poppy seeds
¼ teaspoon Worcestershire sauce
¼ teaspoon sweet paprika
½ cup mild vegetable oil, such as canola
SALAD
⅓ cup walnut halves
1 tablespoon sugar

½ teaspoon ground cinnamon
⅛ teaspoon ground cloves
1 pound fresh spinach, well rinsed, tough stems discarded, and leaves torn into bite-size pieces
¼ pound fresh bean sprouts, rinsed and drained
1 small red onion, thinly sliced (1 cup)
1 pint fresh raspberries or hulled small strawberries

PREP TIME: 25 MIN
COOK TIME: 5 MIN

1. **To make dressing:** In a food processor or blender, combine ½ cup sugar, vinegar, poppy seeds, Worcestershire sauce, paprika, and oil. Process until just blended and thickened slightly. Set aside.

2. Preheat oven to 350°F. Arrange walnuts in a single layer on a baking sheet. In a small bowl, combine 1 tablespoon sugar, cinnamon, and cloves. Sprinkle evenly over walnuts and bake until walnuts are lightly toasted and fragrant, 5 to 7 minutes, shaking pan once.

3. **To make salad:** In a large serving bowl, toss spinach and bean sprouts. Separate onion slices into rings and add to salad.

4. To serve, divide salad mixture among six individual serving plates. Top each serving with raspberries and toasted walnuts. Serve dressing separately. Makes about six 2-cup servings.

1 serving: 331 calories, 4 g protein, 23 g total fat (1.8 g saturated), 31 g carbohydrates, 65 mg sodium, 0 cholesterol, 5 g dietary fiber

ENDIVE, PEAR, AND BLUE CHEESE SALAD WITH BALSAMIC DRESSING

MAKES 4 SERVINGS

This is a particularly interesting salad, a variation of one I had last summer at a country restaurant when I was visiting the covered bridges of Madison County, Iowa. If red Bartlett pears are in season, use them for this salad. Make the dressing ahead so the flavor has time to develop.

BALSAMIC DRESSING
- ¼ cup olive oil
- 3 tablespoons balsamic vinegar
- 2 tablespoons heavy cream
  Salt, optional, and freshly ground black pepper to taste

SALAD
- ⅓ cup walnuts
- 2 large heads Belgian endive
- 2 large red Bartlett pears, cored and thinly sliced
- 2 ounces blue cheese, such as Maytag or Gorgonzola, crumbled (½ cup)
- ½ small red onion, thinly sliced (½ cup)

PREP TIME:
15 MIN

COOK TIME:
5-7 MIN

1. **To make dressing:** In a small bowl, whisk together oil, vinegar, and heavy cream. Taste and add salt, if desired, and pepper. Set aside.
2. Preheat oven to 350°F. Arrange walnuts in a single layer on a baking sheet. Bake until walnuts are lightly toasted and fragrant, 5 to 7 minutes, shaking pan once. Set aside to cool.
3. **To make salad:** Meanwhile, separate endive leaves. Rinse and drain on paper towels. Cut leaves diagonally into thin julienne strips.
4. To serve, arrange endive on 4 individual serving plates. Arrange pear slices over endive. Whisk dressing and spoon over salads. Top each serving with blue cheese, onion slices, and toasted walnuts. Serve immediately. Makes 4 salads.

1 serving: 338 calories, 6 g protein, 26 g total fat (6.7 g saturated), 24 g carbohydrates, 221 mg sodium, 21 mg cholesterol, 5 g dietary fiber

ROMAINE SALAD WITH WARM CHEESE DRESSING

MAKES 6 SERVINGS

In the early nineteenth century, when Western Europeans first settled the central plains of Wisconsin, the land was lauded as ideal for producing the high-quality milk necessary to make cheese. Today there are close to 200 cheese factories in Wisconsin, several of which are operated by cheese producers from France who have found the milk closely resembles that of the French regions that produce Brie and Camembert. Here the rich, creamy cheese is melted to make a warm dressing for the crisp hearts of romaine. Sometimes my market offers these inner hearts already trimmed and bagged together. Other times I purchase more than one head of romaine and reserve the larger outer leaves for another use, such as a Caesar salad, the next day. This is a lovely salad to serve alongside roasted beef, lamb, or pork.

WARM CHEESE DRESSING
- ⅓ cup extra-virgin olive oil
- 1 shallot, minced (1 tablespoon)
- 1 large garlic clove, minced
- 2 tablespoons white wine vinegar
- 1 teaspoon Dijon-style mustard
- 6 ounces ripe Brie or Camembert cheese, at room temperature, rind removed and cheese cut into small pieces

SALAD
- Inner leaves from 2 or 3 medium heads romaine lettuce, rinsed, crisped, and cut into bite-size pieces (6 cups)
- 1 cup Garlic Croutons (see page 47)

PREP TIME: 15 MIN
COOK TIME: 10 MIN

1. **To make dressing:** In a small skillet, warm olive oil over medium-low heat. Add shallot and garlic and sauté until shallot is soft, about 5 minutes. Stir in vinegar and mustard. Add cheese and stir until cheese is melted and mixture is smooth. Keep warm.
2. **To make salad:** Make 1 cup Garlic Croutons. Divide lettuce among 6 individual serving plates and sprinkle with croutons. Pour warm dressing over salads and serve right away. Makes about six 1-cup servings.

1 serving: 283 calories, 8 g protein, 24 g total fat (9.0 g saturated), 9 g carbohydrates, 320 mg sodium, 39 mg cholesterol, 1 g dietary fiber

TOMATO SALAD WITH JALAPEÑO MAYONNAISE

MAKES 8 SERVINGS

Tomatoes just picked from the garden served with my mother's home-made mayonnaise was one of my favorite foods when I was growing up in Kansas. I have fond memories of her using a rotary beater to make the mayonnaise. These days it is much easier to use a food processor. Here I've added some pickled jalapeño peppers to my basic mayonnaise recipe. This salad is terrific with most any grilled meat or fish.

JALAPEÑO MAYONNAISE
- 2 large egg yolks
- 2 tablespoons fresh lemon juice
- 2 tablespoons water
- 1 teaspoon sugar
- ¾ teaspoon salt
- ½ teaspoon dry mustard
- ¼ teaspoon freshly ground black pepper
- ⅛ teaspoon cayenne pepper

- 1 cup mild vegetable oil, such as canola
- 3 tablespoons minced pickled jalapeño chile peppers or to taste

SALAD
- 3 pounds firm ripe tomatoes
- 1 small red onion, thinly sliced and separated into rings (1 cup)
- 8 green leaf lettuce leaves, rinsed and crisped
  Fresh cilantro leaves for garnish, optional

PREP TIME: 15 MIN
COOK TIME: 10 MIN
CHILL TIME: AT LEAST 1 HR

1. **To make mayonnaise:** In top of a double boiler, whisk together egg yolks, lemon juice, water, sugar, salt, mustard, pepper, and cayenne. Cook on low heat over simmering (not boiling) water, stirring constantly, until mixture bubbles in 1 or 2 places and coats the back of a spoon. Remove from water and let stand for 4 minutes. Pour mixture into a food processor or blender. Cover and process until smooth. With motor running, slowly pour oil through feed tube in a thin, steady stream and process until well blended and thickened. Transfer to a small serving bowl. Stir in jalapeño. Cover and chill for at least 1 hour.

2. **To make salad:** Core and slice tomatoes. Arrange lettuce leaves on a large serving platter and top with tomato slices. Scatter the onion rings over the top. Garnish with cilantro leaves. Serve mayonnaise separately. Makes 8 servings.

1 serving: 305 calories, 2 g protein, 29 g total fat (2.4 g saturated), 11 g carbohydrates, 292 mg sodium, 53 mg cholesterol, 2 g dietary fiber

MOLDED CUCUMBER SALAD

MAKES 6 SERVINGS

Cucumbers are a rewarding vegetable for the home gardener. They don't need pampering, and since cucumbers are rapid growers (fifty-five to seventy days), they are suitable for most gardens, even those in the northern regions of the Heartland, where the growing season is short. Here cucumbers, sour cream, and dill are combined to make a refreshing molded salad.

2 medium cucumbers
1 cup small-curd cream-style
   cottage cheese
1 cup sour cream
½ small yellow onion, coarsely
   chopped (¼ cup)
2 tablespoons prepared horseradish
1 6-ounce package lime-flavored gelatin

2 cups boiling water
⅓ cup tarragon vinegar (see page 89)
1 medium celery rib, finely chopped (½ cup)
2 tablespoons minced fresh dill
   or 2 teaspoons dried dill weed
   Thin slices cucumber for garnish, optional
   Cherry tomatoes, stemmed and quartered,
   for garnish, optional

**PREP TIME:
25 MIN

CHILL TIME:
AT LEAST
6 1/2 HR**

1. Lightly oil a 6-cup, preferably fluted, metal mold. Set aside.
2. Peel cucumbers and cut in half lengthwise. Using a small spoon, scoop out and discard seeds. Coarsely shred cucumbers. Drain well in a colander for 10 minutes.
3. Meanwhile, in a food processor or blender, combine cottage cheese, sour cream, onion, and horseradish and process until smooth.
4. In a medium bowl, combine gelatin and boiling water, stirring 2 minutes, until gelatin is dissolved. Stir in vinegar and set aside.
5. Add cottage cheese mixture, shredded cucumber, celery, and dill to gelatin, stirring until blended. Chill for 30 minutes, stirring occasionally.
6. Pour chilled gelatin mixture into the prepared mold. Chill until firm, at least 6 hours.
7. To serve, unmold gelatin (see below) onto a serving platter. Garnish with cucumber slices and cherry tomatoes. Chill until ready to serve. Makes about six 1-cup servings.

1 serving: 247 calories, 9 g protein, 10 g total fat (6.0 g saturated), 33 g carbohydrates, 251 mg sodium, 22 mg cholesterol, 1 g dietary fiber

TO UNMOLD
GELATIN SALADS

At least thirty minutes before serving, select a serving platter that is larger than the diameter of the gelatin mold. Using a small metal spatula or dinner knife, gently loosen the edges of gelatin mixture from the mold. Half-fill a large bowl or sink with warm (not hot) water; dip the mold into water almost up to rim for 5 to 10 seconds. Remove mold from water, pat dry, and shake to loosen gelatin or gently pry gelatin from edge of mold.

Slightly moisten the serving platter with cold water so gelatin can be moved easily after unmolding. Place platter on top of mold and invert. Gently shake, then lift off mold. If the mold doesn't release easily, dip again in warm water. Chill the gelatin until ready to serve.

WARM FIDDLEHEAD SALAD

MAKES 4 SERVINGS

Fiddleheads are young, tightly coiled ferns that are shaped like the scroll of a violin. Indigenous to the northern woods of the Heartland, they are available from April through July, depending on the region. Here they are stir-fried until crisp-tender and served warm, lightly dressed with an herb vinaigrette, for a simple yet sophisticated salad. If fiddleheads aren't in season, you can substitute sugar snap peas.

16 fiddlehead ferns or 16 sugar snap peas
3 cups torn mixed baby lettuces, rinsed and crisped
2 cups torn curly endive leaves (chicory), rinsed and crisped
2 teaspoons minced fresh chives
2 teaspoons minced fresh mint leaves

2 teaspoons minced fresh flat-leaf parsley
¼ cup hazelnut oil or olive oil
2 shallots, minced (2 tablespoons)
3 tablespoons raspberry vinegar or raspberry thyme vinegar (see page 89)
Salt, optional, and freshly ground black pepper to taste

PREP TIME: 15 MIN
COOK TIME: 10 MIN

1. Rinse fiddleheads under cold running water; remove any brown flecks. Drain well and set aside.
2. In a medium bowl, combine lettuces and endive. Divide the mixture among 4 individual serving plates. Set aside. In a small bowl, combine chives, mint, and parsley. Set aside.
3. In a large skillet, heat oil over medium-low heat. Add shallots and sauté until soft, about 3 minutes. Stir in fiddleheads and sauté until fiddleheads are crisp-tender, 3 to 5 minutes. Add vinegar and cook for 30 seconds more.
4. To serve, arrange fiddleheads over lettuce. Sprinkle with fresh herbs. Spoon remaining oil-vinegar mixture in skillet over salads. Serve right away, passing salt, if desired, and pepper at the table. Makes about four 1-cup servings.

1 serving: 154 calories, 2 g protein, 14 g total fat (1.0 g saturated), 7 g carbohydrates, 21 mg sodium, 0 cholesterol, 3 g dietary fiber

SPECIALTY VINEGARS

Expensive to buy but easy to make, flavored vinegars will add distinction and excitement to your salads. Restricted only by the limits of your imagination and the availability of fresh herbs and spices, they can be as simple or complex as you like.

You can recycle pretty bottles and jars to use or purchase bottles in interesting shapes from gourmet kitchenware stores. The procedure is simple: start with a clean, sterilized bottle; fresh herbs and spices; and a good-quality vinegar (white wine vinegar, red wine vinegar, or cider vinegar). If using herbs from your garden, pick them after the morning dew is gone. Clean, if necessary, and pat dry with paper towels, being sure not to bruise the leaves. Loosely fill the bottle with herbs as desired, then fill the bottle with heated vinegar. Let steep until cool. Strain through a fine sieve and discard herbs. Resterilize bottle and place fresh herbs and/or spices in bottom of jar or decorative bottle. Pour vinegar into bottle, seal tightly, and label. The vinegars will be ready to use in one month. Store infused vinegar in a cool, dry, dark place up to six months.

Here are some of my favorite combinations:

Dill Vinegar: 4 large sprigs fresh dill and 2 cups white wine vinegar. Strain, replace sprigs of dill, and add a continuous spiral of rind from 1 lemon.

Italian Salad Vinegar: 2 sprigs fresh oregano, 2 sprigs fresh basil, 1 large bay leaf, 2 cups red or white wine vinegar. Strain and replace sprigs of oregano, basil, and bay leaf.

Opal Basil Vinegar: 3 to 4 sprigs fresh opal basil and 2 cups white wine vinegar. Strain and replace sprigs of basil.

Raspberry Thyme Vinegar: 2 sprigs fresh thyme and 2 cups red wine vinegar. Strain, replace sprigs of thyme, and add 1 cup fresh raspberries and ⅓ cup sugar.

Rosemary Vinegar: 3 sprigs fresh rosemary and 2 cups red wine vinegar. Strain, replace sprigs of rosemary, and add 1 teaspoon fennel seeds.

Tarragon Vinegar: 2 long sprigs fresh tarragon and 2 cups white wine vinegar. Strain, replace sprigs of tarragon, and add 4 peeled, whole shallots.

Tex-Mex Vinegar: 3 sprigs fresh cilantro and 2 cups red or white wine vinegar. Strain, replace sprigs of cilantro, and add 6 small dried chile peppers and 2 peeled, whole garlic cloves.

Thyme and Rosemary Vinegar: 2 sprigs fresh rosemary, 2 sprigs fresh thyme, and 2 cups white wine vinegar. Strain, replace sprigs of rosemary and thyme, and add ½ teaspoon peppercorns.

HEARTLAND SUMMER CORN AND TOMATO SALAD

MAKES 6 SERVINGS

Across the Heartland by midsummer and continuing through to the end of the fall harvest, farmers begin their daily (sometimes twice daily) treks to the local produce stands and farmers' markets with mounds of fresh-picked sweet corn. If the corn is very young and very fresh, it can be used uncooked in this salad. At most, steam the kernels for two to three minutes. Make the dressing ahead so the flavor has time to develop.

RED WINE VINEGAR DRESSING
1 ½ tablespoons red wine vinegar
1 teaspoon Dijon-style mustard
½ teaspoon hot paprika
¼ teaspoon hot pepper sauce
⅓ cup extra-virgin olive oil
  Salt, optional, and freshly ground black pepper to taste

SALAD
6 medium ears fresh-picked white or yellow corn, husked
1 small red onion, finely chopped (½ cup)
3 medium plum tomatoes, chopped (1 cup)
2 cups trimmed arugula leaves or baby spinach leaves, rinsed and crisped
2 cups torn radicchio leaves or shredded red cabbage

PREP TIME: 20 MIN

COOK TIME: 3 MIN (OPTIONAL)

1. **To make dressing:** In a large serving bowl, whisk together vinegar, mustard, paprika, and hot pepper sauce. Slowly add oil, whisking vigorously until well blended. Taste and add salt, if desired, and pepper.

2. **To make salad:** Hold each corn cob vertically over a shallow dish. Using a sharp knife, cut the kernels from the cobs (you should get about 3 cups of corn). If desired, blanch the corn kernels in boiling water until crisp-tender, 2 to 3 minutes. Drain well, plunge into ice water, and drain again.

3. To serve, add corn, onion, and tomatoes to dressing in serving bowl and toss to mix. Add arugula and radicchio and toss again to mix. Makes about six 1 ¼-cup servings.

1 serving: 192 calories, 3 g protein, 13 g total fat (1.8 g saturated), 19 g carbohydrates, 41 mg sodium, 0 cholesterol, 3 g dietary fiber

WARM GRILLED VEGETABLE SALAD

MAKES 4 SERVINGS

Since my kitchen has a built-in grill, I can make this savory salad even during inclement winter months. But the vegetables can also be broiled. While you're grilling the vegetables, also grill some thick slices of a crusty peasant-style or sourdough bread to serve with the salad. I grow basil, rosemary, and sage indoors during the winter, but you can use a pinch of dried herbs if fresh is not available. Crumble the dried herbs between your fingers to release their flavor before adding them to the dressing. Make the dressing ahead so the flavor has time to develop.

DRESSING

- 2 tablespoons white wine vinegar
- 1 large garlic clove, minced
- ⅓ cup olive oil
- 1 tablespoon minced fresh flat-leaf parsley
- 1 teaspoon minced fresh basil leaves
- 1 teaspoon minced fresh sage leaves
- ¼ teaspoon minced fresh rosemary leaves

SALAD

- 1 small Japanese eggplant, trimmed and thinly sliced diagonally into ¼-inch thick slices
- 1 medium yellow onion, peeled and cut into ½-inch-thick slices
- 1 large red bell pepper, seeded and cut into ¼-inch thick wedges
- 1 medium sweet potato, scrubbed, parboiled for 10 minutes, drained, and cut into ¼-inch thick wedges
- 1 medium zucchini, trimmed, cut in half crosswise, and thinly sliced lengthwise into ¼-inch thick slices
- 2 tablespoons olive oil
  Salt, optional, and freshly ground black pepper to taste
- 1 small bunch arugula, well rinsed, trimmed, and drained on paper towels
- 3 tablespoons freshly grated Parmesan cheese

PREP TIME: 25 MIN

COOK TIME: 8–10 MIN

1. **To make dressing:** In a small bowl, whisk together vinegar and garlic. Slowly add oil, whisking vigorously until well blended. Stir in parsley, basil, sage, and rosemary. Set aside.

2. **To make salad:** Start a charcoal or gas grill or preheat broiler. Lightly brush vegetables on both sides with olive oil and season with salt, if desired, and pepper. Grill over medium-hot coals or broil vegetables 4 inches from heat source, turning once or twice, until slightly charred and tender, 8 to 10 minutes.

3. To serve, arrange arugula leaves in a large shallow serving bowl. Top with warm grilled vegetables. Whisk dressing and drizzle over salads. Sprinkle with Parmesan cheese and serve right away. Makes 4 salads.

1 serving: 326 calories, 5 g protein, 27 g total fat (4.3 g saturated), 19 g carbohydrates, 104 mg sodium, 4 mg cholesterol, 3 g dietary fiber

KAREN'S GARLICKY AND SWEET COLESLAW

MAKES 8 SERVINGS

I tasted this delicious coleslaw while photographing another cookbook in this series, Crockery Favorites. *The food stylist, Karen Tack, prepared the garlicky cabbage salad for our lunch—it was so good that I took the leftovers back to the hotel with me for my supper. This recipe comes from Karen's husband, Chris, who works as a chef on a corporate jet. Both had lived in the Midwest, but they didn't meet until years later, while attending culinary school. Chris says he uses whatever cabbage he has on hand from purple to Napa.*

1 medium head cabbage (1 ½ pounds), cored and shredded (6 cups)
1 medium fennel bulb, trimmed, bulb shredded, and leaves chopped (2 cups)
2 large carrots, peeled and shredded (2 cups)
1 large garlic clove

1 teaspoon salt, plus additional for seasoning
1 cup mayonnaise
¼ cup frozen pineapple juice concentrate
1 tablespoon cider vinegar
Freshly ground black pepper to taste
2 tablespoons chopped parsley for garnish

PREP TIME: 15 MIN

1. In a large bowl, combine cabbage, fennel, and carrots.
2. In a medium bowl, using a fork or the side of a chef's knife, mash garlic with salt to form a smooth paste. Stir in mayonnaise, pineapple juice concentrate, and vinegar until well blended.
3. Spoon over cabbage mixture and toss to coat. Taste and add salt, if desired, and pepper. Garnish with chopped parsley. Serve at room temperature or chilled. Makes about eight 1 ¼-cup servings.

1 serving: 243 calories, 2 g protein, 22 g total fat (3.3 g saturated), 11 g carbohydrates, 451 mg sodium, 16 mg cholesterol, 3 g dietary fiber

SUMMER CONFETTI SALAD

MAKES 8 SERVINGS

Here's a great salad to take on a picnic since it can be made well ahead of time. I usually make this with rotini pasta, but you could also use elbow macaroni, penne, or ziti. Maytag blue cheese is a creamy, pungent blue cheese made in Iowa by descendants of the Maytag washing machine founder. Once made, the big wheels of blue cheese are cut into wedges with special cutters that were fashioned from washing machine parts. Available in some specialty cheese shops, Maytag blue cheese is also available by mail order (see Sources, page 142). This salad is lightly dressed. If you prefer a well-dressed salad, double the dressing recipe. Make the dressing ahead so the flavor has time to develop.

BASIL DRESSING
- ⅓ cup chopped fresh basil leaves
- 2 tablespoons balsamic vinegar
- 2 tablespoons red wine vinegar
- 1 large garlic clove, minced
- ½ cup mild vegetable oil, such as canola

SALAD
- 1 pound dried rotini (corkscrew) pasta
- 1 large green bell pepper, seeded and chopped (1 ½ cups)
- 1 medium yellow onion, finely chopped (1 cup)
- 1 4-ounce jar whole pimientos, drained and chopped
- 2 ounces Maytag blue cheese, crumbled (½ cup)
- 1 cup drained pitted large black olives, sliced
- Sprigs fresh basil for garnish, optional

PREP TIME: 20 MIN
COOK TIME: 20 MIN
CHILL TIME: 2 HR. (OPTIONAL)

1. **To make dressing:** In a food processor or blender, combine basil, both vinegars, and garlic and process to form a paste. With motor running, slowly add oil through feed tube in a thin, steady stream until well blended. Transfer to a small bowl and set aside.

2. **To make salad:** Cook pasta according to package directions. Drain well, quickly rinse under cold running water, and drain again.

3. In a large bowl, combine pasta, bell pepper, onion, pimentos, blue cheese, and olives. Gently toss to mix. To serve at room temperature, whisk dressing, pour over salad, and toss to coat. To serve chilled, dress salad just before serving.

4. Transfer pasta salad to a large serving bowl or platter. Garnish with fresh basil sprigs. Makes about eight 1 ½-cup servings.

1 serving: 393 calories, 10 g protein, 18 g total fat (2.6 g saturated), 48 g carbohydrates, 230 mg sodium, 5 mg cholesterol, 3 g dietary fiber

BEAN MEDLEY

MAKES 8 SERVINGS

We grew several varieties of fresh beans in our Kansas garden—old-fashioned Kentucky Wonders, which climbed willow poles lashed together to form a tepee, yellow wax bush beans, and Fordhook bush lima beans. It wasn't until about five years ago that I was introduced to fresh fava beans, a flat broad bean that resembles a very large lima bean. Combined with some simple seasonings, then stuffed into hollowed-out tomatoes, these beans make a terrific salad that will stay fresh for hours, perfect to serve as part of a buffet.

SALAD

- 2 pounds fresh beans of mixed varieties such as green beans, wax beans, fresh (or frozen) lima beans, and shelled fava beans
- 1 medium red onion, thinly sliced (1 ½ cups)
- ¼ pound fresh goat cheese, crumbled (½ cup)
  Salt, optional, and freshly ground black pepper to taste
- 4 large firm ripe tomatoes
- 1 small head red leaf lettuce, leaves rinsed and crisped, for garnish, optional
  Chopped fresh basil leaves for garnish, optional

HERB MUSTARD DRESSING

- 3 tablespoons sherry vinegar or white wine vinegar
- 1 large garlic clove, minced
- 1 tablespoon minced fresh basil leaves or 1 teaspoon dried, crumbled
- 1 tablespoon minced fresh oregano leaves or 1 teaspoon dried, crumbled
- 1 teaspoon minced fresh thyme leaves or ¼ teaspoon dried, crumbled
- 1 teaspoon prepared horseradish
- ½ teaspoon Dijon-style mustard
- ½ cup olive oil

PREP TIME: 30 MIN
COOK TIME: 15 MIN

1. **To make salad:** Trim stem ends of green and wax beans. Cut beans into 1 ½-inch pieces. Blanch in boiling water until crisp-tender, 3 to 4 minutes. Plunge into ice water, drain well, and set aside.

2. Shell lima beans. Blanch in boiling water until just tender, about 5 minutes. Plunge into ice water, drain well, and set aside.

3. Remove fava beans from the pods. Blanch in boiling water for 5 minutes. Drain, rinse under running cold water, and drain again. Using your fingernail, break the outer skin of the fava bean and squeeze the bean out between your forefinger and thumb.

4. In a large bowl, combine beans, onion, and goat cheese. Taste and add salt, if desired, and pepper. Set aside.

5. Cut tomatoes in half crosswise. Scoop out and discard pulp and seeds. Invert shells on paper towels to drain. Set aside.

6. **To make dressing:** In a small bowl, whisk together vinegar, garlic, herbs, horseradish, and mustard. Slowly add oil, whisking vigorously until well blended. Pour dressing over bean mixture and toss gently to coat. Fill tomato shells with about 1 cup of the bean mixture.

7. To serve, arrange lettuce leaves on a large serving platter and place filled tomatoes on lettuce. Sprinkle each serving with chopped basil. Makes 8 servings.

1 serving: 274 calories, 9 g protein, 19 g total fat (5.5 g saturated), 19 g carbohydrates, 75 mg sodium, 15 mg cholesterol, 5 g dietary fiber

KANSAS LAYERED 24-HOUR SALAD

MAKES 10 SERVINGS

This recipe comes from my sister-in-law Helen, who grew up in Newton, Kansas. I've taken some liberties, adding some updated ingredients and fresh herbs to her recipe with satisfying results. A favorite of potluck suppers during the 1960s, layered salads are even better today since more quality produce is available year-round. If fresh water chestnuts aren't available, substitute drained canned water chestnuts. Layer the ingredients in your prettiest clear glass straight-sided bowl for an impressive presentation, worthy of a party buffet. This salad is lightly dressed.

SALAD

4 cups torn mixed greens such as Belgian endive, radicchio, and romaine, rinsed and crisped

1 medium red onion, thinly sliced (1 ½ cups)

2 medium celery ribs, thinly sliced (1 cup)

½ pound fresh radishes, trimmed and thinly sliced (1 ½ cups)

1 small cauliflower, cut into small florets (2 cups)

6 fresh water chestnuts, peeled and thinly sliced (½ cup)

1 10-ounce package frozen baby peas, thawed and drained

¼ cup chopped fresh basil leaves

2 tablespoons chopped fresh mint leaves

1 tablespoon chopped fresh thyme leaves

3 hard-cooked large eggs, peeled and sliced

6 slices bacon, crisply cooked, drained, and crumbled

1 cup shredded Swiss cheese (¼ pound)

½ cup freshly grated Parmesan cheese

2 medium tomatoes, thinly sliced

DRESSING

½ cup mayonnaise

½ cup sour cream

1 large garlic clove, minced
Salt, optional, and freshly ground black pepper to taste

PREP TIME: 30 MIN
CHILL TIME: 24 HR OR AT LEAST 8 HR

1. **To make salad:** Arrange greens in the bottom of a 4-quart glass serving bowl. Cover with a layer of onion, then celery, radishes, cauliflower, water chestnuts, and peas. Sprinkle herbs over peas. Layer the egg slices, then bacon and Swiss cheese.

2. **To make dressing:** In a small bowl, mix mayonnaise, sour cream, and garlic until well blended. Taste and add salt, if desired, and pepper.

3. Spread dressing evenly over top of salad, sealing the edges. Sprinkle with Parmesan cheese and cover tightly with plastic wrap. Chill for 24 hours or at least 8 hours.

4. To serve, arrange tomato slices over top of salad. Using a serving spoon and fork, lift out salad, marking sure each serving includes some of each layer. Makes about ten 1 ¼-cup servings.

1 serving: 268 calories, 12 g protein, 20 g total fat (7.0 g saturated), 13 g carbohydrates, 339 mg sodium, 93 mg cholesterol, 3 g dietary fiber

OLD-FASHIONED RED POTATO SALAD

MAKES 8 SERVINGS

This is the potato salad that we always took on picnics, along with a basket filled with my mother's fried chicken, jars of homemade sweet lime pickles, jugs of lemonade, and a couple of fresh-baked fruit pies. If traveling with this salad, be sure it stays well chilled until serving.

3 pounds tiny new red-skinned potatoes, scrubbed
2 medium celery ribs with some leaves, thinly sliced (1 ½ cups)
1 medium red onion, chopped (1 cup)
⅓ cup chopped dill pickle
3 large hard-cooked eggs, peeled
¾ cup mayonnaise

1 ½ tablespoons prepared mustard
1 ½ tablespoons cider vinegar
1 tablespoon celery seed
   Salt, optional, and freshly ground black pepper to taste
1 small head Boston lettuce, leaves rinsed and crisped for garnish, optional
   Sweet paprika for garnish, optional

**PREP TIME:
20 MIN
COOK TIME:
15 MIN
CHILL TIME:
AT LEAST
3 HR**

1. Depending on their size, cut the potatoes into halves or quarters. Boil potatoes in water to cover until tender, about 15 minutes. Drain well and let cool.

2. In a large bowl, combine potatoes, celery, onion, and pickle. Chop two hard-cooked eggs and add to salad. Slice remaining egg and set aside.

3. In a small bowl, mix mayonnaise, mustard, vinegar, and celery seed until well blended. Add to potato mixture and toss to coat. Taste and add salt, if desired, and pepper. Cover and chill for at least 3 hours.

4. To serve, arrange lettuce leaves in a large serving bowl. Spoon potato salad into center. Arrange reserved sliced egg over top and garnish with a generous sprinkling of paprika. Makes about eight 1½-cup servings.

1 serving: 332 calories, 7 g protein, 19 g total fat (3.2 g saturated), 35 g carbohydrates, 293 mg sodium, 92 mg cholesterol, 4 g dietary fiber

NORTH WOODS WILD RICE SALAD

MAKES 8 SERVINGS

Wild rice is the long-grain of a marsh grass. Once harvested the grain is dried on sheets of birch bark, winnowed, then packaged for sale. Look for wild rice in specialty food stores, natural foods stores, and large supermarkets. It's also available by mail order (see Sources, page 142). Make the dressing ahead so the flavor has time to develop.

DRESSING

- 2 tablespoons fresh lemon juice
- 2 tablespoons sherry vinegar or white wine vinegar
- 1 teaspoon Dijon-style mustard
- 1 shallot, minced (1 tablespoon)
- ⅛ teaspoon hot pepper sauce
- ½ cup olive oil

SALAD

- 2 cups wild rice
- 6 cups water
- ½ cup pecan halves
- 1 ½ cups fresh peas or 1 10-ounce package frozen tiny peas, thawed
- 1 medium celery rib, thinly sliced (½ cup)
- 1 small red onion, finely chopped (½ cup)
- 2 tablespoons drained capers
  Salt, optional, and freshly ground black pepper to taste
  Thin red onion rings for garnish, optional

1. **To make dressing:** In a small bowl, whisk together lemon juice, vinegar, mustard, shallot, and hot pepper sauce. Slowly add oil, whisking vigorously until well blended. Set aside.
2. **To make salad:** In a medium saucepan, bring wild rice and water to a boil. Reduce heat, cover, and simmer until rice is tender, 50 to 55 minutes. Drain well. Cool rice slightly.

PREP TIME: 20 MIN
COOK TIME: 55 MIN
CHILL TIME: AT LEAST 2 HR

3. Meanwhile, preheat oven to 350°F. Arrange pecans on a baking sheet. Bake until pecans are lightly toasted and fragrant, 5 to 7 minutes, shaking pan once. Set aside to cool.
4. In a large serving bowl, combine wild rice, peas, celery, onion, and capers. Whisk dressing and pour over salad. Toss to mix and coat. Taste and add salt, if desired, and pepper. Cover and chill for at least 2 hours.
5. To serve, add pecans and toss again. Garnish with red onion rings. Makes about eight 1¼-cup servings.

1 serving: 338 calories, 8 g protein, 19 g total fat (2.3 g saturated), 37 g carbohydrates, 106 mg sodium, 0 cholesterol, 4 g dietary fiber

WARM ROOT VEGETABLE SALAD

MAKES 6 SERVINGS

Root vegetables are a staple food for farm families during the cold-weather season because they keep for months in a cool, dry place. At my grandparents' farm, there was a root cellar beneath the kitchen of the house and a cave near the windmill. Both were used to store the summer's harvest of carrots, parsnips, potatoes, onions, rutabagas, sweet potatoes, and turnips. This is a wonderful winter vegetable salad, the hot bacon dressing complementing the earthy flavors of the vegetables. It goes beautifully with roast chicken or turkey.

SALAD

- 2 medium carrots, peeled and cut into 1-inch cubes
- 1 medium sweet potato, peeled and cut into 1-inch cubes
- 2 medium parsnips, peeled and cut into 1-inch cubes
- 2 small turnips, peeled and cut into 1-inch cubes
- 1 medium russet potato, peeled and cut into 1-inch cubes

Salt, optional, and freshly ground black pepper to taste

HOT BACON DRESSING

- 4 slices bacon, cut into 1-inch pieces
- 3 tablespoons olive oil
- 2 tablespoons white wine vinegar
- 2 green onions, white part only, finely chopped (¼ cup)
- ½ teaspoon fresh thyme leaves or ⅛ teaspoon dried, crumbled

PREP TIME: 30 MIN
COOK TIME: 30 MIN

1. **To make salad:** Bring a large saucepan of water to a boil. Add carrots and sweet potato and cook until just tender, 10 to 15 minutes. Using a slotted spoon, remove vegetables and set aside. In same pan, cook parsnips, turnips, and potato in boiling water until just tender, 10 to 15 minutes. Drain. Combine vegetables in a large serving bowl.

2. **To make dressing:** Meanwhile, in a large skillet, cook bacon over medium heat until crisp. Using a slotted spoon, remove to paper towels to drain. Pour off all but 2 tablespoons of bacon drippings from skillet. Add oil and stir until heated through. Stir in vinegar, green onions, and thyme. Remove from heat.

3. To serve, pour warm dressing over salad. Add reserved bacon pieces and toss gently to mix. Taste and add salt, if desired, and pepper. Serve right away. Makes about six 1-cup servings.

1 serving: 217 calories, 3 g protein, 14 g total fat (3.8 g saturated), 21 g carbohydrates, 134 mg sodium, 8 mg cholesterol, 4 g dietary fiber

BEET AND APPLE SALAD

MAKES 6 SERVINGS

This is a very pretty salad, certain to brighten up a fall or early winter menu. Serve it over a mixture of Belgian endive and crisp watercress for an appealing presentation. Roasting intensifies the flavor and color of fresh beets. Once roasted and peeled, the beets are ready to use in any recipe. They can be roasted ahead and stored in a sealed container in the refrigerator until ready to use. Pomegranates are in season from the end of September to mid-December. If unavailable, substitute red seedless grapes.

SALAD

4 medium fresh beets (about 1 pound), scrubbed and trimmed, 1-inch stem left intact

2 cups cubed fresh pineapple or 1 20-ounce can pineapple chunks packed in juice, drained

1 large red-skinned apple, such as Ida Red, Rome, or Jonathan, cored and sliced (1 ½ cups)

½ cup pomegranate seeds or seedless red grape halves

1 medium head Belgian endive, leaves separated, rinsed, and crisped

1 bunch watercress, large stems discarded, leaves rinsed and crisped
Salt, optional, and freshly ground black pepper to taste

HONEY-DIJON DRESSING

3 tablespoons cider vinegar

1 tablespoon Dijon-style mustard

1 tablespoon minced red onion

2 teaspoons honey

⅓ cup olive oil or mild vegetable oil, such as canola

**PREP TIME:
20 MIN
COOK TIME:
1 1/2 HR**

1. **To make salad:** Preheat oven to 350°F. Wrap each beet in a square of aluminum foil. Place on a baking sheet and roast until tender, about 1 ½ hours. Remove from oven. When cool enough to handle, unwrap beets and slip off skins. Cut beets into thin slices and set aside.
2. In a large serving bowl, mix pineapple, apple, and pomegranate seeds. Add endive and watercress and toss to mix.
3. **To make dressing:** In a small bowl, whisk together vinegar, mustard, onion, and honey. Slowly add oil, whisking vigorously until well blended.
4. Add beets to salad. Whisk dressing and pour over salad. Gently toss to mix and coat. Taste and add salt, if desired, and pepper. Makes about six 1-cup servings.

1 serving: 208 calories, 3 g protein, 13 g total fat (1.7 g saturated), 24 g carbohydrates, 136 mg sodium, 0 cholesterol, 5 g dietary fiber

SEEDING A POMEGRANATE

If you work under water when freeing the seeds of a pomegranate, you won't get the bright crimson juice all over you and the counter. Cut the pomegranate into quarters. Place in a deep bowl of water. While working under water, gently remove the seeds from the membrane. Discard the shell and membranes. Drain the seeds on paper towels.

MACARONI AND CHEESE SALAD

MAKES 8 SERVINGS

This is my favorite recipe for macaroni salad, a terrific side dish to serve with grilled hamburgers. It was given to me years ago by Mike Roy, a friend who hosted a syndicated radio talk show featuring hometown recipes across the country. A native of North Dakota, Mike claimed the secret to his recipe is that the vinaigrette is poured over the macaroni while it's still hot. This salad is lightly dressed. If you prefer a well-dressed salad, increase the mayonnaise to 1 cup.

DRESSING

- 2 tablespoons white wine vinegar
- ½ tablespoon fresh lemon juice
- ½ teaspoon Worcestershire sauce
- ½ teaspoon salt
- ¼ teaspoon freshly ground black pepper
- ⅛ teaspoon dry mustard
- ¼ cup olive oil

SALAD

- 2 cups dried elbow or shell macaroni
- ¼ pound sharp Cheddar cheese, cut into ½-inch cubes (1 cup)
- 3 large celery ribs, thinly sliced (3 cups)
- 1 medium red onion, finely chopped (1 cup)
- ¼ cup sliced pimiento-stuffed olives
- 2 tablespoons sweet pickle relish
- 2 tablespoons chopped dill pickle
- ½ cup mayonnaise
- 1 ½ teaspoons prepared mustard
  Salt, optional, and freshly ground
  black pepper to taste
  Baby lettuces, leaves rinsed and crisped,
  for garnish, optional
  Chopped fresh dill for garnish, optional

PREP TIME: 15 MIN

COOK TIME: 15 MIN

CHILL TIME: AT LEAST 4 HR

1. **To make dressing:** In a small bowl, whisk together vinegar, lemon juice, Worcestershire sauce, salt, pepper, and mustard. Slowly add oil, whisking vigorously until well blended.

2. **To make salad:** Cook macaroni according to package directions. Drain well. Transfer to a large bowl. Pour dressing over hot macaroni and toss to coat. Cover and chill for at least 2 hours.

3. Add cheese, celery, onion, olives, relish, pickle, mayonnaise, and mustard to pasta. Gently toss to mix. Cover and chill for at least 2 hours more.

4. To serve, taste salad and add salt, if desired, and pepper. Spoon into center of a large serving platter. Surround with baby lettuces and garnish with chopped dill. Makes about eight 1 ½-cup servings.

1 serving: 340 calories, 8 g protein, 23 g total fat (5.7 g saturated), 26 g carbohydrates, 489 mg sodium, 23 mg cholesterol, 2 g dietary fiber

BROCCOLI SALAD WITH SWEET AND SOUR RAISIN DRESSING

MAKES 6 SERVINGS

When I was growing up in the Heartland, broccoli usually came frozen in a box. It was one of the few vegetables that my dad didn't grow. When fresh broccoli occasionally appeared in the grocery store, it was expensive— too expensive for my mother, who was a frugal shopper. Fortunately fresh broccoli is now available at reasonable prices in supermarkets year-round. The peak season is October through April. Here broccoli is tossed with bell peppers for a delicious salad. To prevent the vegetables from discoloring, don't add the dressing until the last minute.

SALAD

1 pound fresh broccoli spears
1 medium red bell pepper, seeded and cut into thin julienne strips (1 ½ cups)
1 medium yellow bell pepper, seeded and cut into thin julienne strips (1 ½ cups)
¼ cup sunflower seeds

SWEET AND SOUR RAISIN DRESSING

⅓ cup cider vinegar
¼ cup mild vegetable oil, such as canola
3 tablespoons light brown sugar
1 large garlic clove, minced
1 teaspoon Dijon-style mustard
1 teaspoon freshly ground black pepper
⅛ teaspoon hot pepper sauce
¼ cup golden raisins

PREP TIME: 20 MIN
COOK TIME: 20 MIN

1. **To make salad:** Cut broccoli tops into 1 ½-inch florets. Peel broccoli stems and cut into thin slices. Blanch broccoli stems in boiling water until bright green and crisp-tender, about 5 minutes. Add the florets for the last minute. Plunge broccoli into ice water and drain well.

2. In a large serving bowl, mix broccoli and bell peppers.

3. In a medium nonstick skillet, toast sunflower seeds over medium heat, shaking pan often, until seeds are fragrant and lightly toasted, 3 to 4 minutes. Remove from heat and set aside.

4. **To make dressing:** In a small saucepan, combine vinegar, oil, sugar, garlic, mustard, pepper, and hot pepper sauce. Bring mixture to a boil over medium-high heat, whisking constantly. Reduce heat and add raisins. Cook, stirring constantly, until raisins are plumped and heated through, about 3 minutes.

5. Pour hot dressing over broccoli mixture and toss to coat. Sprinkle with toasted sunflower seeds. Toss again and serve right away. Makes about six 1-cup servings.

1 serving: 192 calories, 4 g protein, 13 g total fat (1.0 g saturated), 19 g carbohydrates, 46 mg sodium, 0 cholesterol, 4 g dietary fiber

MIXED GRAIN SALAD WITH FETA DRESSING

MAKES 6 SERVINGS

I can buy the grains and dried cherries needed for this salad in my supermarket, but you may need to purchase them at a natural foods store. Dried cherries are also available by mail order (see Sources, page 142). Quinoa is an ancient grain that's recently become popular throughout the Heartland. Here it's combined with couscous, dried fruit, and feta cheese for a salad to complement almost any roasted meat or fowl.

SALAD

- ¼ cup currants
- 3 tablespoons pine nuts
- 2 cups water
- ½ cup quinoa, rinsed
- ½ cup couscous
- 8 dried apricot halves, finely chopped
- ½ cup dried cherries
- 1 medium celery rib, thinly sliced (½ cup)
- 1 small red onion, finely chopped (½ cup)
  Lettuce leaves, rinsed and crisped

FETA DRESSING

- 2 tablespoons fresh lemon juice
- 1 tablespoon grated lemon rind
- 1 tablespoon minced fresh flat-leaf parsley
- 1 tablespoon minced fresh mint leaves
- ¼ teaspoon sweet paprika
- 5 tablespoons olive oil
- ¼ cup crumbled feta cheese (1 ounce)
  Salt, optional, and freshly ground
  black pepper to taste

PREP TIME: 25 MIN
COOK TIME: 20 MIN

1. **To make salad:** In a small bowl, soak currants in hot water to cover for 15 minutes. Drain well and squeeze dry.

2. Meanwhile, in a small skillet, toast pine nuts over medium heat, stirring frequently, until golden brown, 3 to 5 minutes.

3. In a medium saucepan, bring water to a boil. Add quinoa. Reduce heat, cover, and simmer for 15 minutes. Remove from heat and stir in couscous. Cover and let stand for 5 minutes. Drain if necessary.

4. In a large bowl, mix apricots, cherries, currants, celery, and onion.

5. **To make dressing:** In a small bowl, whisk together lemon juice, lemon rind, parsley, mint, and paprika. Slowly add oil, whisking vigorously until well blended. Stir in feta cheese. Taste and add salt, if desired, and pepper.

6. Add grain mixture to apricot mixture. Toss gently to mix. Whisk dressing, pour over salad, and toss to coat.

7. To serve, line a serving platter with lettuce leaves. Add pine nuts to salad and gently toss to mix. Spoon salad into center of platter. Makes about six 1-cup servings.

1 serving: 284 calories, 6 g protein, 15 g total fat (2.6 g saturated), 35 g carbohydrates, 71 mg sodium, 4 mg cholesterol, 4 g dietary fiber

POULTRY, SEAFOOD, AND MEAT SALADS

IN THE HEARTLAND TODAY, main-dish salads go far beyond the chef's salad and fruit plate that once were the only choices on restaurant menus. Today you'll find salads containing a substantial portion of meat, poultry, or seafood, served over a bed of greens, with vegetables or pasta providing an interesting contrast of texture and taste.

These are recipes where presentation is important and culinary artistry comes into play since the salads should be composed and arranged for visual appeal as well as flavor impact. The flavors range from hot and pungent to refreshing and sweet. Here you'll find substantial salads to satisfy the "meat and potatoes" members of your family as well as lighter, healthy salads to impress the ladies at a club luncheon. When it's too hot to cook indoors, fire up the barbecue for a grilled steak or duck salad. If you're in a hurry, you can easily purchase ingredients for the smoked turkey or roast beef salad from the delicatessen.

HOT GERMAN POTATO SALAD WITH GRILLED SAUSAGES

MAKES 6 SERVINGS

My husband, David, is German — his father immigrated to Danzig, South Dakota, from a German colony in the Ukraine, and his mother was born in Berlin. I've adapted this recipe from one I found in his mother's recipe file — it's quite delicious, especially when served with some grilled knockwurst or bratwurst. Add sauerkraut and some German mustard and you have an easy meal. I like to use tiny new white potatoes for this recipe. If you have a kitchen garden, you should be able to start harvesting the thin-skinned potatoes by mid- or late June.

2 pounds tiny new potatoes, scrubbed
2 pounds fully cooked German sausages such as knockwurst, bratwurst, or Polish sausage (kielbasa)
5 slices bacon
2 large celery ribs, thinly sliced (2 cups)
1 medium red onion, chopped (1 cup)

1 medium green bell pepper, seeded and chopped (1 cup)
¼ cup cider vinegar
1 teaspoon sugar
Salt, optional, and freshly ground black pepper to taste
2 tablespoons chopped parsley for garnish, optional

PREP TIME: 20 MIN
COOK TIME: 40 MIN

1. Boil potatoes in water to cover until tender, about 15 minutes. Drain well and set aside. When cool enough to handle, slice potatoes about ¼ inch thick.

2. Meanwhile, start a charcoal or gas grill or preheat broiler. Arrange sausages on a lightly oiled grill rack or broiler pan. Grill over medium-hot coals or broil 4 to 6 inches from heat source, turning frequently, until well browned on all sides and heated through, 7 to 10 minutes. Transfer sausages to a carving board and cut diagonally into ½-inch thick slices. Keep warm.

3. In a large skillet, cook bacon over medium heat until crisp. Using a slotted spoon, remove bacon to paper towels to drain. Set aside. Add celery, onion, and bell pepper to skillet and sauté until vegetables are soft, about 5 minutes. Add vinegar, sugar, and sliced potatoes. Toss gently to coat evenly. Taste and add salt, if desired, and pepper.

4. Transfer mixture to a large serving bowl. Arrange sausages on top. Crumble bacon and sprinkle on top. Garnish with chopped parsley and serve immediately. Makes about six 2-cup servings.

1 serving: 716 calories, 24 g protein, 53 g total fat (19.5 g saturated), 36 g carbohydrates, 1,702 mg sodium, 100 mg cholesterol, 4 g dietary fiber

GRILLED STEAK AND ASPARAGUS SALAD WITH CILANTRO DRESSING

MAKES 8 SERVINGS

Here's a terrific meal-in-one salad to satisfy hearty eaters. Don't assemble the ingredients until just before serving.

SALAD

2 ½ pounds boneless beef loin strip steak or top sirloin steak, cut 1 inch thick
Salt, optional, and freshly ground black pepper to taste
1 pound fresh asparagus spears
16 small new potatoes, scrubbed and quartered
1 8-ounce package frozen baby ears of corn or 1 can (about 12 ounces), drained
8 cups torn romaine or leaf lettuce, rinsed and crisped
1 pint cherry tomatoes, stemmed and cut in half
Sprigs fresh cilantro for garnish, optional

CILANTRO DRESSING

½ cup loosely packed fresh cilantro leaves
¼ cup freshly grated Parmesan cheese
2 large garlic cloves, minced
2 tablespoons pine nuts
⅛ teaspoon salt
⅛ teaspoon freshly ground black pepper
1 ½ tablespoons olive oil
½ cup mayonnaise

PREP TIME: 25 MIN
COOK TIME: 35 MIN

1. **To make salad:** Start a charcoal or gas grill or preheat broiler. Season steak with salt and pepper. Grill over medium-hot coals or broil 4 to 6 inches from heat source until medium-rare, about 5 minutes on each side. Transfer steak to a carving board and let stand for 5 minutes. Cut steak diagonally into thin slices.

2. Meanwhile, break off and discard white ends of asparagus. Bring a large skillet of water to a boil. Add asparagus and boil gently, uncovered, until crisp-tender, about 5 minutes. Drain well, rinse under cold running water, and drain again.

3. Boil potatoes in water to cover until tender, about 10 minutes. Drain well and cool.

4. Cook frozen corn according to package directions. Drain well and cool.

5. **To make dressing:** In a food processor, combine cilantro, Parmesan cheese, garlic, pine nuts, salt, and pepper. Process for 15 seconds. With motor running, slowly add oil through feed tube until well blended. Transfer mixture to a small bowl. Whisk in mayonnaise until well blended.

6. To serve, arrange lettuce on a large serving platter. Arrange steak, asparagus, potatoes, corn, and tomatoes over lettuce. Garnish with cilantro sprigs. Whisk dressing and serve on the side. Makes 8 servings.

1 serving: 456 calories, 37 g protein, 26 g total fat (6.6 g saturated), 19 g carbohydrates, 257 mg sodium, 90 mg cholesterol, 4 g dietary fiber

TORTILLA TACO SALAD

MAKES 4 SERVINGS

The flour tortillas for this taco salad are spritzed with fresh lime juice, then sprinkled with some Mexican spices and baked in a 450°F oven until crispy. To get the shell shape, the tortillas are draped over an inverted metal mixing bowl during the baking time. The result is a crisp tortilla shell without the muss and fuss (not to say calories) that comes with frying the tortilla in a huge pot of oil. The tortilla shells can be baked ahead of time and stored in an airtight plastic container for up to 1 week. If you're in a hurry, you can serve the salad on top of a pile of purchased tortilla chips with good results.

MARINATED PORK

- 2 pork tenderloins (10 ounces each), trimmed of excess fat
- 1 small yellow onion, minced (½ cup)
- 3 tablespoons chopped fresh oregano leaves or 1 tablespoon dried, crumbled
- 2 large garlic cloves, minced
- 1 teaspoon freshly ground black pepper
- ⅓ cup fresh lemon juice (2 large lemons)
- 1 tablespoon olive oil

SALSA DRESSING

- 1 cup sour cream
- ¾ cup bottled salsa, spicy or mild
- 3 tablespoons minced red onion
- 1 tablespoon finely chopped cilantro or fresh flat-leaf parsley

TORTILLA SHELLS

- 1 teaspoon dried oregano leaves, crumbled
- ¾ teaspoon chili powder
- ¼ teaspoon salt
- ½ cup fresh lime juice, strained (4 to 5 large limes)
- 4 flour tortillas (10 to 13 inches in diameter)

FILLING

- 1 15-ounce can black beans, heated and drained
- 1 large head iceberg lettuce, shredded (8 cups)
- 4 medium tomatoes, chopped (4 cups)
- 1 cup shredded Cheddar cheese (¼ pound)
- ¾ cup shredded Monterey Jack cheese (3 ounces)
- ¼ cup sliced pitted black olives
- 4 green onions, white part and 1 inch green, thinly sliced (½ cup)
- ¼ cup chopped fresh cilantro leaves
- 1 large ripe avocado, preferably Hass, pitted, peeled, and thinly sliced
  Miniature red and yellow peppers for garnish, optional

PREP TIME: 1 HR
COOK TIME: 15 MIN
STAND TIME: 5 MIN

1. **To marinate pork:** Place pork tenderloins in a zipper-type plastic bag. In a small bowl, combine onion, oregano, garlic, pepper, lemon juice, and olive oil. Pour over pork, seal bag, and marinate in the refrigerator for at least 30 minutes.

2. **To make the salsa dressing:** Meanwhile, in a small serving bowl, mix sour cream, salsa, onion, and cilantro until well blended. Cover and chill until ready to use.

3. **To bake tortilla shells:** Preheat oven to 450°F. Invert a 1-quart metal mixing bowl (or ovenproof glass bowl) on top of a large baking sheet. Drape a 12-inch square of aluminum foil over the bottom of the bowl. In a small bowl, combine oregano, chili powder, and salt. Set aside. Place the lime juice in a sprayer or atomizer. Mist 1 tortilla with the juice until soft and pliable. Sprinkle with ¼ teaspoon oregano mixture. Quickly drape tortilla slightly off center over the bowl. Bake in oven until lightly browned and firm enough to hold its shape, about 4 to 5 minutes. Carefully lift tortilla shell off bowl and invert, cup side up, onto another baking sheet. If the sides of the shell need support, crumple a narrow strip of aluminum foil and gently press the foil against the shell to support the sides. Bake for another 2

Bake for another 2 to 3 minutes, until crisp and nicely browned. Remove from oven and cool on a wire rack. Repeat process until all tortilla shells are baked. Set aside. (If making ahead, store cooled tortilla shells in a tightly sealed container for up to 1 week.)

4. Start a charcoal or gas grill or preheat broiler. Remove pork from marinade and grill over medium-hot coals or broil 4 inches from heat source for 10 to 12 minutes, until internal temperature reaches 140°F, turning once and basting occasionally with marinade. Remove pork to a carving board and let stand for 5 minutes. Cut pork into thin slices. In a medium bowl, toss pork slices with heated black beans. Keep warm.

5. To serve, place tortilla shells on individual serving plates. Mound 2 cups shredded lettuce in each shell. Top with pork and bean mixture, tomatoes, and shredded cheeses. Sprinkle with olives, green onions, and cilantro. Arrange avocado slices on top. Garnish with miniature peppers. Serve dressing separately to spoon over salads. Makes 4 taco salads.

1 serving: 933 calories, 58 g protein, 49 g total fat (21.6 g saturated), 69 g carbohydrates, 1,617 mg sodium, 158 mg cholesterol, 13 g dietary fiber

POTATO, HAM, AND PEA SALAD WITH FRESH DILL

MAKES 6 SERVINGS

This colorful potato salad is a favorite of the Heartland picnic crowd. Since it doesn't contain any mayonnaise, it holds up well in hot weather. Take along a plastic bag of crisp fresh greens to serve as a bed for the salad. Assemble the dish on site. Another time, serve the salad warm as a casual weeknight supper entree with a cup of Roasted Onion Soup (page 33) and some warm biscuits or muffins.

SALAD

1 ½ pounds small red-skinned potatoes, scrubbed

1 pound boneless smoked fully cooked ham, sliced 1 inch thick

2 cups shelled fresh peas or 1 10-ounce package frozen peas, thawed and drained

2 medium celery ribs, thinly sliced (1 cup)

1 medium red onion, chopped (1 cup)

2 tablespoons chopped fresh dill or 2 teaspoons dried dill weed
  Green loose-leaf lettuce for garnish, optional

HORSERADISH-DILL DRESSING

2 tablespoons red wine vinegar

1 large garlic clove, minced

½ teaspoon Dijon-style mustard

½ teaspoon prepared horseradish

⅛ teaspoon freshly ground black pepper or to taste

⅓ cup olive oil

PREP TIME: 25 MIN
COOK TIME: 25 MIN

1. **To make salad:** Boil the potatoes in water to cover until tender, about 15 minutes. Drain well. When cool enough to handle, thinly slice potatoes into a large bowl.

2. Meanwhile, cut the ham into 1-inch cubes.

3. If using fresh peas, blanch in boiling water until crisp-tender, about 3 minutes. Drain well, rinse under cold running water, and drain again. (Do not precook frozen peas.)

4. Add peas, ham, celery, and onion to bowl.

5. **To make dressing:** In a small bowl, whisk together vinegar, garlic, mustard, horseradish, and pepper. Slowly add oil, whisking vigorously until well blended.

6. To serve, pour dressing over potato mixture. Sprinkle with dill and toss gently to coat. Line a large serving bowl with lettuce leaves and mound salad in the center. Serve at room temperature or chilled. Makes about six 2-cup servings.

1 serving: 323 calories, 18 g protein, 15 g total fat (2.9 g saturated), 31 g carbohydrates, 939 mg sodium, 36 mg cholesterol, 5 g dietary fiber

BLT IN A BOWL
WITH GARLIC CROUTONS

MAKES 4 SERVINGS

Bacon, lettuce, and tomato sandwiches have always been a favorite at my house. My mother would sometimes bake bacon in the oven with brown sugar and chopped nuts to use as a topping for an asparagus casserole. When I found the recipe for the topping in her old cooking notebook, I knew I had the beginnings of a terrific salad. Be sure to have fresh basil on hand when you make this salad.

SALAD
8 slices bacon
3 tablespoons dark brown sugar
1 teaspoon unbleached all-purpose flour
⅓ cup chopped pecans
1 medium head Boston lettuce, leaves rinsed and crisped
1 small head Belgian endive, leaves separated and rinsed
1 pint cherry tomatoes, stemmed and cut in half

⅓ cup finely chopped fresh basil leaves
½ recipe Garlic Croutons (page 47)
Salt, optional, and freshly ground black pepper to taste

MUSTARD VINAIGRETTE
2 tablespoons red wine vinegar
1 tablespoon fresh lemon juice
3 tablespoons minced red onion
½ teaspoon dry mustard
⅓ cup walnut oil or mild vegetable oil, such as canola

PREP TIME: 15 MIN
COOK TIME: 30 MIN

1. **To make salad:** Preheat oven to 350°F. Arrange bacon slices in a single layer on a broiler pan, as close together as possible without overlapping. In a small bowl, combine brown sugar, flour, and pecans. Sprinkle evenly over bacon. Bake until bacon is crisp and nicely browned, about 30 minutes. (Do not turn.) Using a wide spatula, carefully transfer to paper towels to drain, keeping the pecan pieces on top. Set aside. Make ½ recipe Garlic Croutons.

2. Meanwhile, tear lettuce leaves into bite-size pieces. Thinly slice endive leaves crosswise.

3. In a large serving bowl, combine lettuce, endive, tomatoes, and basil. Crumble bacon and add with the pecans bits to bowl.

4. **To make dressing:** In a small bowl, whisk together vinegar, lemon juice, onion, and mustard. Slowly add oil, whisking vigorously until well blended. Pour dressing over salad and gently toss to coat.

5. Sprinkle with croutons. Serve, passing salt, if desired, and pepper at the table. Makes about four 1½-cup servings.

1 serving: 439 calories, 8 g protein, 36 g total fat (7.3 g saturated), 24 g carbohydrates, 350 mg sodium, 22 mg cholesterol, 3 g dietary fiber

ROAST BEEF SALAD

MAKES 6 SERVINGS

When it's too hot to cook, make this salad with roast beef from the delicatessen. It's also a terrific way to use up the rest of Sunday's roast. Make the dressing ahead so the flavor has time to develop.

TARRAGON DRESSING
1 tablespoon Dijon-style mustard
1 tablespoon minced fresh tarragon leaves
  or 1 teaspoon dried, crumbled
1 large garlic clove, minced
3 tablespoons red wine vinegar
½ cup olive oil
¼ cup dry red wine
¼ cup bottled chili sauce

SALAD
2 pounds thinly sliced cooked roast beef
1 medium red bell pepper, seeded and cut
  into thin julienne strips (1 ½ cups)
2 large plum tomatoes, diced (1 cup)
1 small red onion, thinly sliced (1 cup)
  Salt, optional, and freshly ground
  black pepper to taste
1 large bunch arugula, trimmed, rinsed,
  and crisped
2 large hard-cooked eggs, peeled
  and chopped

PREP TIME:
30 MIN
CHILL TIME:
AT LEAST
3 HR

1. **To make dressing:** In a small bowl, whisk together mustard, tarragon, garlic, and vinegar. Slowly add oil, whisking vigorously until well blended. Whisk in wine and chili sauce.
2. **To make salad:** In a large serving bowl, combine roast beef, bell pepper, tomatoes, and onion.
3. Pour dressing over roast beef mixture. Toss gently to coat. Taste and add salt, if desired, and pepper. Cover and chill for at least 3 hours or overnight.
4. To serve, arrange arugula on a large serving platter. Pile beef mixture on top and sprinkle with chopped egg. Makes 6 servings.

1 serving: 504 calories, 48 g protein, 29 g total fat (6.2 g saturated), 11 g carbohydrates, 343 mg sodium, 175 mg cholesterol, 1 g dietary fiber

WILTED GREENS WITH CHICKEN AND CRANBERRIES

MAKES 4 SERVINGS

Wisconsin's number-one fruit crop, cranberries are an industry that has been passed down by Wisconsin families since the mid-1800s. Fresh cranberries are available for only a short time each fall; freeze an extra bag or two so you'll have cranberries on hand for this salad throughout the year. If I'm grilling chicken for a meal, I cook extra for this salad. But it can also be purchased in the delicatessen section of most large supermarkets. I like to include some arugula and spinach in the greens mixture; otherwise it's what's ready in the garden or looks best at the market.

SALAD

- 6 cups torn mixed salad greens, rinsed and crisped
- 1 pound fully cooked skinless, boneless chicken breasts, cut into thin julienne strips

DRESSING

- ½ cup fresh or frozen cranberries, picked over and rinsed
- 2½ tablespoons sugar

- 4 slices bacon, cut into 1-inch pieces
- 1 small green bell pepper, seeded and minced (½ cup)
- 2 shallots, minced (2 tablespoons)
- 1 large garlic clove, minced
- 2 tablespoons balsamic vinegar
- ¼ cup mild vegetable oil, such as canola
- 1 teaspoon chili powder
- ¼ teaspoon dry mustard

PREP TIME:
20 MIN
COOK TIME:
15 MIN

1. **To make salad:** Divide salad greens among 4 serving plates. Top with chicken strips. Set aside.

2. **To make dressing:** In a food processor, process cranberries until finely chopped. Add sugar and process for 30 seconds. Set aside.

3. In a large skillet, cook bacon over medium heat until crisp. Using a slotted spoon, remove to paper towels to drain. Crumble bacon and set aside.

4. Add bell pepper, shallots, and garlic to bacon drippings in skillet and sauté until soft, about 5 minutes. Whisk in vinegar, oil, chili powder, and mustard. Stir in reserved cranberries. Cook, stirring frequently, for 1 minute.

5. Spoon warm mixture over each salad. Garnish each serving with reserved bacon. Makes four salads.

1 serving: 501 calories, 39 g protein, 31 g total fat (7.0 g saturated), 16 g carbohydrates, 269 mg sodium, 112 mg cholesterol, 2 g dietary fiber

GRILLED DUCK SALAD

This delicious salad has a lot going for it: the smoky flavor of grilled duck breast; sweet, juicy peaches; and the saltiness of finely chopped ham. Wild duck is a favorite game of sports hunters from the northern regions of the Heartland to the plains of Kansas and Oklahoma. Commercially, ducks are raised in several Midwestern states, primarily Wisconsin. If duck breast isn't available, you can substitute chicken or turkey breast. The dressing is made with hazelnut oil, although you could also use walnut or light olive oil. Make the dressing ahead so the flavor has time to develop. See page 9 for the photograph of this dish.

HAZELNUT VINAIGRETTE
- ⅓ cup red wine vinegar
- 1 tablespoon fresh lemon juice
- 1 large garlic clove, minced
- ½ teaspoon dry mustard
- ½ teaspoon freshly ground black pepper
- ⅔ cup hazelnut oil, walnut oil, or light olive oil

SALAD
- 2 boneless duck breasts (about 8 ounces each)
  Salt, optional, and freshly ground black pepper to taste

- 2 tablespoons balsamic vinegar
- 2 large garlic cloves, minced
- 1 teaspoon minced fresh thyme leaves or ¼ teaspoon dried, crumbled
- ½ teaspoon minced fresh rosemary or ⅛ teaspoon dried, crumbled
- 3 large ripe peaches, peeled, halved, and pitted
- 1 medium head Bibb lettuce, rinsed and crisped
- 2 ounces smoked fully cooked ham, finely chopped
- 1 recipe Spicy Hazelnuts (page 21)

PREP TIME: 30 MIN
COOK TIME: 15 MIN

1. **To make dressing:** In a small bowl, whisk together red wine vinegar, lemon juice, garlic, mustard, and pepper. Slowly add oil, whisking vigorously until well blended and slightly thickened. Set aside.

2. **To make salad:** Remove skin and all visible fat from duck breasts. Rinse and pat dry. Season with salt, if desired, and pepper. In a small bowl, mix balsamic vinegar, garlic, thyme, and rosemary to form a paste. Spread mixture over duck breasts and let stand for 10 minutes.

3. Start a charcoal or gas grill or preheat broiler. Place duck breasts on a lightly oiled grill rack or broiler pan 4 to 6 inches from heat source. Grill over medium-hot coals or broil for 5 minutes. Turn duck breasts and add peach halves to the grill. Continue to grill for another 5 to 7 minutes, turning peaches once. (Duck will still be slightly pink in the center; cut to test.)

4. Meanwhile, divide lettuce among 4 individual serving plates. Cut peaches into slices, fan on once side of lettuce, and sprinkle with chopped ham.

5. Transfer duck to a carving board and let stand for 5 minutes. Cut duck diagonally into thin slices. Arrange duck slices next to peaches on each plate. Sprinkle duck with spicy hazelnuts. Whisk dressing and drizzle over salads. Makes 4 salads.

1 serving: 680 calories, 28 g protein, 57 g total fat (8.7 g saturated), 19 g carbohydrates, 297 mg sodium, 110 mg cholesterol, 3 g dietary fiber

SMOKED TURKEY SALAD

A lot of Midwestern cooks own a smoker for making brisket, ribs, and chicken or turkey. If you have the good fortune to have apple wood chips, by all means use them. If you don't own a smoker, purchase smoked turkey at your favorite delicatessen.

⅔ cup long-grain white rice
1 ⅓ cups water

HERB DRESSING
¼ cup red wine vinegar
1 teaspoon dry mustard
1 teaspoon Worcestershire sauce
1 tablespoon chopped fresh dill
  or 1 teaspoon dried dill weed
1 teaspoon fresh thyme leaves
  or ¼ teaspoon dried, crumbled
⅔ cup mild vegetable oil, such as canola
  Salt, optional, and freshly ground
  black pepper to taste

SALAD
¾ pound smoked turkey, cut into thin strips
  (2 cups)
1 medium green bell pepper, seeded and diced
  (1 cup)
2 medium celery ribs with leaves, diced (1 cup)
¼ cup red seedless grapes, halved
  Inner leaves from 1 small head romaine
  lettuce, rinsed and crisped
4 green onions, white part and 1 inch green
  tops, thinly sliced (½ cup) for garnish,
  optional
3 slices bacon, crisply cooked, drained,
  and crumbled for garnish, optional

PREP TIME:
35 MIN
CHILL TIME:
AT LEAST
2 HR

1. In a medium saucepan, bring rice and water to a boil. Reduce heat, cover, and simmer until rice is tender and liquid is absorbed, about 15 minutes.

2. **To make dressing:** Meanwhile, in a small bowl, whisk together vinegar, mustard, Worcestershire sauce, dill, and thyme. Slowly add oil, whisking vigorously until well blended. Taste and add salt, if desired, and pepper.

3. **To make salad:** In a large serving bowl, combine rice, turkey, bell pepper, celery, and grapes. Whisk dressing, pour over mixture, and gently toss to coat. Cover and chill for at least 2 hours.

4. To serve, arrange lettuce leaves around edge of large serving platter. Spoon turkey and rice mixture into center. Garnish with green onions and bacon. Makes about four 1 ¾-cup servings.

1 serving: 583 calories, 22 g protein, 40 g total fat (3.6 g saturated), 35 g carbohydrates, 1,249 mg sodium, 41 mg cholesterol, 2 g dietary fiber

GRILLED CITRUS CHICKEN SALAD

MAKES 4 SERVINGS

Chicken marinated in citrus juice and garlic with fresh fruit and baby greens tastes far heartier than a mere chicken and fruit salad. The raspberry vinaigrette adds a refreshing flavor to the chicken and fruits.

SALAD

- 2 whole skinless, boneless chicken breasts (½ pound each)
- ½ cup fresh orange juice (1 large orange)
- ½ cup fresh grapefruit juice (1 small grapefruit)
- 3 large garlic cloves, minced
- 2 teaspoons grated peeled fresh ginger
- 1 teaspoon minced fresh rosemary leaves or ¼ teaspoon dried, crumbled
- 2 tablespoons mild vegetable oil, such as canola
  Salt, optional, and freshly ground black pepper to taste

RASPBERRY VINAIGRETTE

- ⅓ cup raspberry vinegar or raspberry thyme vinegar (page 89)
- 1 shallot, minced (1 tablespoon)
- 1 tablespoon minced fresh cilantro or flat-leaf parsley
- 2 teaspoons honey
- ½ cup hazelnut oil or mild vegetable oil, such as canola
  Salt, optional, and freshly ground black pepper to taste

- 2 large navel oranges
- 1 large pink grapefruit
- 8 cups baby lettuce leaves, rinsed and crisped
- ½ cup fresh raspberries

PREP TIME: 30 MIN + AT LEAST 1 HR TO MARINATE CHICKEN

COOK TIME: 15 MIN

1. **To make salad:** Rinse chicken breasts and pat dry. In a medium bowl, whisk together orange juice, grapefruit juice, garlic, ginger, and rosemary. Slowly whisk in oil. Sprinkle chicken with salt, if desired, and pepper and arrange in a nonreactive dish. Pour the juice mixture over chicken and turn to coat. Cover with plastic wrap and marinate in the refrigerator for at least 1 hour or up to 12 hours, turning the chicken every 15 minutes during the first hour.

2. Meanwhile, peel and remove the white pith from oranges and grapefruit. Thinly slice the fruit crosswise. Set aside.

3. Start a charcoal or gas grill or preheat broiler. Remove chicken from marinade. Set aside. Pour marinade into a small saucepan and bring to a boil over high heat. Boil, uncovered, for 2 minutes. Remove from heat.

4. Place chicken on a lightly oiled grill rack or broiler pan 4 to 6 inches from heat source. Grill over medium-hot coals or broil chicken until golden brown and no longer pink in center, about 5 minutes per side, basting occasionally with marinade. Transfer chicken to a carving board and thinly slice across the grain. Keep warm.

5. **To make vinaigrette:** In a small bowl, whisk together vinegar, shallot, cilantro, and honey. Slowly add hazelnut oil, whisking vigorously until well blended. Taste and add salt, if desired, and pepper. Set aside.

6. To serve, line a large serving platter with lettuce. Arrange orange and grapefruit slices over lettuce and top with sliced chicken. Whisk dressing and drizzle over salad. Top with raspberries. Makes 4 servings.

1 serving: 509 calories, 29 g protein, 33 g total fat (2.7 g saturated), 28 g carbohydrates, 85 mg sodium, 66 mg cholesterol, 4 g dietary fiber

TUNA AND PASTA SALAD

MAKES 6 SERVINGS

Today's Midwestern cooks occasionally like to wilt the lettuce or greens for a salad. Here a fresh-tasting tuna and pasta salad is served on a bed of baby lettuces that have been wilted in a mellow-tasting walnut vinaigrette. If you don't own a hand grater for the Parmesan cheese, you can use a vegetable peeler to shave it. This salad is lightly dressed. If you prefer a well-dressed salad, double the dressing recipe, drizzling the extra dressing over the tuna-pasta mixture.

SALAD

- ¾ pound dried tube-shaped pasta such as penne or ziti
- 1 12-ounce can water-packed white albacore tuna, drained and flaked into large chunks
- 1 15-ounce can artichoke hearts, drained and cut into quarters
- 1 medium carrot, peeled and shredded (¾ cup)
- ¼ pound fresh mushrooms, thinly sliced (1 ½ cups)
- 1 small red onion, thinly sliced (1 cup)

- 6 cups mixed baby lettuce leaves, rinsed and crisped
- 3 ounces Parmesan cheese in 1 piece

WALNUT OIL VINAIGRETTE

- 2 tablespoons fresh lemon juice
- 1 tablespoon cider vinegar
- ¾ teaspoon Dijon-style mustard
- ⅛ teaspoon Worcestershire sauce
- ½ cup walnut oil
- Salt, optional, and freshly ground black pepper to taste

PREP TIME: 20 MIN
COOK TIME: 20 MIN

1. **To make salad:** Cook pasta according to package directions. Drain well, rinse under cold running water, and drain again.

2. Put pasta in a large bowl and mix gently with tuna. Add artichokes, carrot, mushrooms, and onion. Toss gently to mix. Set aside.

3. **To make vinaigrette:** In a small bowl, whisk together lemon juice, vinegar, mustard, and Worcestershire sauce. Slowly add oil, whisking vigorously until well blended. Taste and add salt, if desired, and pepper.

4. In a large skillet, heat vinaigrette over medium heat until barely warm, about 2 to 3 minutes. Put lettuces in a medium bowl. Pour warm dressing over greens and toss to coat lightly.

5. Arrange wilted greens on a large serving platter. Spoon pasta salad over greens. Shave Parmesan cheese over salad. Makes about six 2 ½-cup servings.

1 serving: 536 calories, 27 g protein, 24 g total fat (4.5 g saturated), 52 g carbohydrates, 568 mg sodium, 29 mg cholesterol, 3 g dietary fiber

SEAFOOD SALAD WITH WHITE BEANS

MAKES 6 SERVINGS

Michigan is bean country— more than 300 million acres of fertile land are planted with beans that will be dried or processed and canned. The world's largest producer of navy beans (small white beans), Michigan also has close to 3,000 growers of asparagus. So it seemed appropriate to combine the two in this special salad. Large sea scallops are readily available in fish markets and larger supermarkets from mid-fall to the end of the fresh asparagus season. Shrimp are always available, either fresh or frozen. If you can't get scallops, use all shrimp. This salad is lightly dressed. If you prefer a well-dressed salad, double the dressing recipe.

FRESH HERB DRESSING
3 tablespoons red wine vinegar
1 tablespoon fresh lemon juice
2 teaspoons Dijon-style mustard
2 tablespoons chopped fresh herbs such as chives, parsley, and tarragon
⅓ cup olive oil
  Salt, optional, and freshly ground black pepper to taste

SALAD
1 pound small fresh asparagus spears, preferably white
1 small eggplant, cut into 1-inch thick slices
2 fresh portobello mushrooms, cleaned and cut into 1-inch thick slices
3 tablespoons olive oil
1 pound sea scallops, rinsed and patted dry
½ pound uncooked medium shrimp, peeled and deveined
3 tablespoons fresh lemon juice (1 large lemon)
4 cups torn mixed salad greens such as red leaf, romaine, arugula, and radicchio, rinsed and crisped
1 15-ounce can navy beans, drained
1 small tomato, chopped (½ cup)

PREP TIME: 25 MIN
COOK TIME: 25 MIN

1. **To make dressing:** In a small bowl, whisk together vinegar, 1 tablespoon lemon juice, mustard, and herbs. Slowly add oil, whisking vigorously until well blended. Taste and add salt, if desired, and pepper. Set aside.

2. **To make salad:** Break off and discard woody ends from asparagus. Blanch spears in a skillet of boiling water until crisp-tender, about 2 minutes. Drain well and transfer to a plate. Drizzle with 2 tablespoons of dressing. Set aside.

3. Start a charcoal or gas grill or preheat broiler. Brush eggplant and mushroom slices with some oil. Grill over medium-hot coals or broil until nicely browned on both sides, about 10 to 12 minutes. Set aside.

4. Meanwhile, thread scallops onto skewers. Thread shrimp onto additional skewers. (If using wooden skewers, soak in water for 30 minutes before using to prevent burning.) Lightly brush scallops and shrimp with remaining oil. Grill or broil 4 to 6 inches from heat source, turning once, until scallops and shrimp are opaque throughout, 5 to 7 minutes for scallops and 3 to 4 minutes for shrimp. Remove from skewers to a plate. Sprinkle with 3 tablespoons lemon juice and set aside.

5. To serve, divide salad greens among 4 large individual serving plates. Arrange asparagus, grilled eggplant and mushrooms, grilled scallops and shrimp, and ⅓ cup beans over each serving. Sprinkle with chopped tomato. Whisk dressing and drizzle over salads. Serve any remaining dressing separately. Makes 4 salads.

1 serving: 358 calories, 23 g protein, 21 g total fat (2.9 g saturated), 23 g carbohydrates, 375 mg sodium, 78 mg cholesterol, 6 g dietary fiber

WARM SHRIMP CAESAR SALAD

MAKES 4 SERVINGS

Although Caesar salad is believed to have been invented in 1924 by a restaurateur in Tijuana, Mexico, the salad has been a favorite of Midwesterners for a long time. In going through my mother's Wichita, Kansas, church and community cookbooks from the 1950s and early 1960s, I found that recipes for Caesar salad were always included. And now, according to reported restaurant sales from the National Restaurant Association, Caesar salad is the number-one salad of the nation. Although not authentic (it lacks the one-minute egg as a health precaution), here's a version that goes well with grilled shrimp (or chicken) to make a whole meal.

SALAD

- 3 tablespoons fresh lemon juice (1 large lemon)
- 1 teaspoon Dijon-style mustard
- ¼ teaspoon fresh thyme leaves or ⅛ teaspoon dried, crumbled
- 12 jumbo uncooked shrimp (about 1 pound), peeled and deveined, tails intact
- 1 large head romaine lettuce, rinsed, crisped, and torn into bite-size pieces
- ¼ cup freshly grated Parmesan cheese
- ½ recipe Garlic Croutons (page 47)

CAESAR DRESSING

- ¾ cup olive oil
- ¼ cup red wine vinegar
- 4 anchovy fillets, drained and chopped
- 2 large garlic cloves, minced
- 1 tablespoon fresh lemon juice
- 2 teaspoons Dijon-style mustard
- 1 teaspoon Worcestershire sauce
- 1 cup freshly grated Parmesan cheese (3 ounces)
- Salt, optional, and freshly ground black pepper to taste

PREP TIME: 25 MIN
COOK TIME: 6 MIN

1. **To make salad:** In a medium nonreactive bowl, whisk together the 3 tablespoons lemon juice, 1 teaspoon mustard, and thyme. Add shrimp and toss gently to coat. Cover and let stand for 15 minutes, turning once.

2. Start a charcoal or gas grill or preheat broiler. Thread 3 shrimp onto each of 4 skewers. (If using wooden skewers, soak in water for 30 minutes before using to prevent burning.) Grill over medium-hot coals or broil 4 to 6 inches from heat source, turning once, until pink, about 3 minutes per side. Keep warm.

3. **To make dressing:** In a food processor or blender, combine olive oil, vinegar, anchovies, garlic, 1 tablespoon lemon juice, 2 teaspoons mustard, and the Worcestershire sauce. Process until smooth. Add 1 cup Parmesan cheese and process for 15 seconds longer. Taste and add salt, if desired, and pepper.

4. Put lettuce in a large serving bowl. Add half of prepared dressing. Toss to mix and coat. Add ¼ cup Parmesan cheese, croutons, and remaining dressing as needed to coat lightly. Toss again.

5. To serve, divide salad among 4 individual serving plates. Arrange shrimp on top of each serving. Serve right away. Makes 4 salads.

1 serving: 738 calories, 41 g protein, 57 g total fat (14.7 g saturated), 16 g carbohydrates, 1,121 mg sodium, 212 mg cholesterol, 2 g dietary fiber

FRUIT SALADS

THE HEARTLAND IS RICH WITH native fruit. From the first stalks of rhubarb in early spring, there's a rapid succession of fruits—tart and sweet cherries; assorted berries ranging from sweet blueberries and strawberries to tart cranberries; pale gold apricots; luscious peaches and plums; juicy pears; several varieties of grapes; refreshingly sweet melons; and more than a dozen varieties of crisp apples.

Using fruit in salads dates back to early pioneer cooks, who sweetened wild berries with honey to serve as a side dish with roasted game and poured heavy cream over chunks of apples, pears, and wild grapes for an early version of fruit salad.

Here you'll find recipes for a variety of fresh fruit salads. The dressings are light to let the natural fruit flavors star. There are recipes suitable for seasonal barbecues and picnics. Other salads such as the Molded Waldorf Salad and Frozen Cranberry Snow will add a festive note to holiday celebrations or can be served as a light fall luncheon entree. All show off the natural beauty and flavor of the fruit.

PRAIRIE FRUIT SALAD

MAKES 8 SERVINGS

The rage of the fifties, this salad (also known as 5-cup salad) showed up at family gatherings and church potlucks throughout the Midwest. This updated version has more fruits and makes a spectacular salad.

1 cup fresh blueberries, rinsed and drained on paper towels

1 medium red-skinned apple such as Red Delicious or Ida Red, cored and coarsely chopped (1 cup)

¼ pound seedless red grapes, halved (1 cup)

1 large navel orange, peeled, sectioned, and coarsely chopped (1 cup)

1 cup fresh or canned pineapple chunks, drained

1 cup plain sour cream

1 tablespoon honey

2 teaspoons peeled and grated fresh ginger

1 small head leaf lettuce, leaves rinsed and crisped

1 large ripe banana, peeled and sliced (1 cup)

1 cup walnuts, coarsely chopped

PREP TIME: 25 MIN

CHILL TIME: AT LEAST 3 HR

1. In a large bowl, combine blueberries, apple, grapes, orange, and pineapple. Set aside.
2. In a small bowl, mix sour cream, honey, and ginger until well blended. Spoon sour cream mixture over fruit and toss gently to coat. Cover and chill for at least 3 hours.
3. To serve, line a serving bowl with lettuce leaves. Stir banana and walnuts into fruit mixture. Spoon salad into center. Makes about eight 1-cup servings.

1 serving: 239 calories, 4 g protein, 16 g total fat (5.0 g saturated), 26 g carbohydrates, 22 mg sodium, 13 mg cholesterol, 4 g dietary fiber

SUMMERTIME FRUIT SALAD WITH HONEY-LIME DRESSING

MAKES 8 SERVINGS

I can remember spending hours on my knees picking berries in my dad's half-acre strawberry patch. Other summer fruits followed in quick succession—red cherries, gooseberries, plums, peaches, pears, grapes and apples. In the fields watermelons and cantaloupes were ripening. A visit to one of our other farms would bring additional fruits needing to be put up: currants, crab apples, mulberries, papaws, persimmons, wild grapes, and wild blackberries. This lovely summer salad highlights my favorite fruits, topped with a lime dressing spiked with a splash of rum.

SALAD

1 cup fresh blackberries
1 cup fresh blueberries
1 cup fresh raspberries
1 cup fresh strawberries, hulled
2 cups bite-size cantaloupe chunks
2 cups bite-size honeydew melon chunks
2 cups bite-size watermelon chunks

HONEY-LIME DRESSING

1 cup crème fraîche (page 25)
2 tablespoons fresh lime juice
2 tablespoons dark rum, optional
1 teaspoon grated lime rind
½ teaspoon sweet paprika
Fresh mint leaves for garnish, optional

PREP TIME: 30 MIN

CHILL TIME: AT LEAST 2 HR

1. **To make salad:** Rinse berries and drain on paper towels. Depending on their size, cut strawberries in halves or quarters.
2. In a large serving bowl, combine berries and melons. Toss to mix. Cover and chill for at least 2 hours.
3. **To make dressing:** Meanwhile, in a small bowl, mix crème fraîche, lime juice, rum, lime rind, and paprika until well blended. Cover and chill until ready use.
4. To serve, pour dressing over fruit and toss to coat. Garnish with fresh mint leaves. Makes about eight 1 ¼-cup servings.

1 serving: 166 calories, 2 g protein, 9 g total fat (5.4 g saturated), 20 g carbohydrates, 23 mg sodium, 27 mg cholesterol, 3 g dietary fiber

CANTALOUPE, TOMATO, AND AVOCADO SALAD WITH HOT CHILE DRESSING

MAKES 8 SERVINGS

When my sister-in-law Gloria first served this salad, I loved its dramatic color and flavor contrasts. Over the years I've experimented with the dressing until I developed this one. This is a salad that I frequently take to potluck picnics, and it never fails to make a hit. This salad is lightly dressed. If you prefer a well-dressed salad, double the dressing recipe.

SALAD

- 1 large ripe cantaloupe, peeled, seeded, and cut into 1½-inch cubes (4 cups)
- 2 medium tomatoes, coarsely chopped (2 cups)
- 2 medium ripe avocados, preferably Hass, pitted, peeled, and sliced
- 8 green loose-leaf lettuce leaves, rinsed and crisped for garnish, optional

HOT CHILE DRESSING

- ¼ cup fresh lemon juice (2 medium lemons)
- 2 teaspoons honey
- 2 teaspoons minced fresh cilantro
- 2 teaspoons minced jalapeño chile pepper
- 2 teaspoons minced fresh flat-leaf parsley
- ½ teaspoon ground cumin

1. To make salad: In a large bowl, combine cantaloupe, tomatoes, and avocados. Toss gently to mix.

2. To make dressing: In a small bowl, whisk together lemon juice, honey, cilantro, jalapeño, parsley, and cumin until well blended. Pour dressing over salad and toss gently to coat. Cover and chill for at least 2 hours.

3. To serve, line a large serving bowl or platter with lettuce leaves. Spoon salad into center. Makes about eight 1-cup servings.

PREP TIME: 25 MIN

CHILL TIME: AT LEAST 2 HR

1 serving: 116 calories, 2 g protein, 7 g total fat (1.1 g saturated), 14 g carbohydrates, 17 mg sodium, 0 cholesterol, 3 g dietary fiber

MIXED FALL FRUIT SALAD

MAKES 6 SERVINGS

Native persimmons grow wild in several Heartland states. They are easily found in the southern regions of Indiana and along the riverbanks of the Mississippi in Missouri. If picked before the first frost, the tangerine-size fruit is very sour, but once touched by cold weather, it becomes incredibly sweet. Native persimmons are rarely sold fresh. Commercially they are available only after being processed into pulp and sold either fresh, frozen, or canned. Asian varieties are readily available in produce stands and supermarkets in autumn and early winter. At other times of the year, persimmons are imported from South America. Here they combine with apples and goat cheese for a showy salad. The production of goat cheese is a relatively new but thriving industry in Wisconsin.

HONEY-MUSTARD
DRESSING

3 tablespoons mild vegetable oil
3 tablespoons cider vinegar
1 tablespoon honey
2 teaspoons Dijon-style mustard

SALAD

3 medium well-ripened fresh persimmons
2 large red-skinned apples such as
Red Delicious, Cortland, or Prairie Spy,
cored and sliced (2 cups)

1 tablespoon fresh lemon juice
1 log-shaped package (6 ounces) fresh
goat cheese
4 cups torn mixed salad greens,
rinsed and crisped
Salt, optional, and freshly ground
black pepper to taste

**PREP TIME:
20 MIN
COOK TIME:
2–3 MIN**

1. **To make dressing:** In a small bowl, whisk together oil, vinegar, honey, and mustard until well blended. Set aside.

2. **To make salad:** Peel persimmons and cut into wedges, removing any seeds. Set aside. In a small bowl, toss apple slices with lemon juice. Set aside.

3. Preheat broiler. Cut goat cheese crosswise into 4 rounds and place on a baking sheet. Broil 3 to 4 inches from heat source until lightly browned, about 2 to 3 minutes.

4. To serve, divide salad greens among 4 individual serving plates. Fan apple slices and persimmon wedges over lettuce. Place 1 goat cheese round on each serving. Whisk dressing and drizzle over salads. Serve, passing salt, if desired, and pepper at the table. Makes 4 salads.

1 serving: 242 calories, 7 g protein, 16 g total fat (6.4 g saturated), 21 g carbohydrates, 198 mg sodium, 22 mg cholesterol, 2 g dietary fiber

BERRY AND PRETZEL SALAD

MAKES 4 SERVINGS

In talking with my Midwestern friends, I've come across several recipes for a molded pretzel and strawberry-raspberry salad that has become quite popular throughout the Heartland. I thought the combination unlikely, but when I tried it I found it delicious, although quite sweet. In my version the salad is not molded, but otherwise the ingredients are much the same, just put together in a different way so the overall taste is lighter and more refreshing. Serve this salad at the height of the berry season, when you can pick or purchase giant strawberries with long stems for the best visual effect.

SALAD

- 1 cup small salted bow-knot pretzels, coarsely crushed
- ¼ cup (½ stick) butter, melted
- 1 tablespoon sugar
- 1 3-ounce package cream cheese, at room temperature
- 2 ounces Gorgonzola or other blue cheese, at room temperature
- 12 very large strawberries with long stems attached, rinsed and drained on paper towels

DRESSING

- 3 tablespoons raspberry vinegar or raspberry thyme vinegar (page 89)
- 1 shallot, minced (1 tablespoon)
- ⅓ cup mild vegetable oil, such as canola

- 4 cups torn mixed salad greens, rinsed and crisped
- ½ cup fresh raspberries, rinsed and drained on paper towels
  Salt, optional, and freshly ground black pepper to taste

PREP TIME: 20 MIN
COOK TIME: 10 MIN
CHILL TIME: AT LEAST 1 HR

1. **To make salad:** Preheat oven to 350°F. In a small bowl, combine pretzels, butter, and sugar. Spread mixture into a 13 x 9-inch baking pan and bake for 10 minutes, stirring once. Remove from oven and let cool.

2. In a small bowl, mix cream cheese and Gorgonzola until smooth and well blended. Cut 1 strawberry in half lengthwise, slightly off center. Spread 2 teaspoons of cheese mixture on cut side of one half. Cover with remaining half to re-form berry shape. Repeat with remaining strawberries. Place filled berries on a plate, cover, and chill for at least 1 hour.

3. **To make dressing:** In a small bowl, whisk together vinegar, shallot, and oil. Set aside.

4. To serve, divide salad greens among 4 individual serving plates. Arrange 3 filled berries over greens. Scatter raspberries around strawberries. Whisk dressing and drizzle over salads. Sprinkle with baked pretzels. Serve with salt, if desired, and pepper. Makes 4 salads.

1 serving: 503 calories, 8 g protein, 41 g total fat (17.1 g saturated), 28 g carbohydrates, 637 mg sodium, 65 mg cholesterol, 4 g dietary fiber

TANGY LEMON-LIME MOLD

MAKES 8 SERVINGS

This salad offers a refreshing contrast to spicy entrees. It's also an impressive salad to serve for a buffet, unmolded onto a cake pedestal. Be sure to chop the cabbage very fine. The gelatin mold can also be made with reduced-fat mayonnaise and plain low-fat yogurt instead of sour cream. Lemon and lime layers are made and chilled separately, then combined.

LEMON LAYER

1 3-ounce package lemon-flavored gelatin
1 cup boiling water
1 6-ounce can frozen lemonade concentrate, thawed
2 cups peeled grapefruit sections, chopped
2 tablespoons grated white onion

LIME LAYER

1 3-ounce package lime-flavored gelatin
1 teaspoon salt
1 cup boiling water
1 tablespoon white wine vinegar
½ teaspoon Worcestershire sauce
½ cup mayonnaise
½ cup sour cream
1 cup finely chopped cabbage
1 small red bell pepper, seeded and minced (½ cup)
¼ cup sliced pimiento-stuffed olives
Mixed salad greens, rinsed and crisped for garnish, optional

PREP TIME: 40 MIN

CHILL TIME: AT LEAST 5 1/4 HR

1. **To make lemon layer:** In a medium bowl, mix lemon-flavored gelatin and boiling water, stirring 2 minutes until gelatin is completely dissolved. Add lemonade concentrate and chill until slightly thickened, about 15 minutes. Fold in grapefruit and onion. Spoon into a lightly oiled 2-quart metal mold. Chill until almost firm, about 1 hour.

2. **To make lime layer:** In a medium bowl, mix lime-flavored gelatin and salt with boiling water, stirring until gelatin is completely dissolved. Add vinegar and Worcestershire sauce. Chill until slightly thickened, about 15 minutes. Using a rubber spatula, gently and thoroughly fold in mayonnaise, sour cream, cabbage, bell pepper, and olives. Spoon mixture over lemon layer. Chill until firm, at least 4 hours.

3. To serve, unmold onto a serving platter (see page 86). Arrange salad greens around gelatin. Makes about eight 1¼-cup servings.

1 serving: 277 calories, 3 g protein, 15 g total fat (3.6 g saturated), 36 g carbohydrates, 486 mg sodium, 15 mg cholesterol, 1 g dietary fiber

MOLDED WALDORF SALAD WITH CRANBERRY DRESSING

MAKES 6 SERVINGS

Perfect for fall dinners, this molded version of the classic apple salad is sure to please the whole family. You could also make this salad with chopped red Bartlett pears instead of apples.

SALAD

- 1 3-ounce package lemon-flavored gelatin
- 1 ¼ cups boiling water
- ¾ cup ginger ale
- 2 large red-skinned apples such as Ida Red, Rome, or Jonathan, cored
- 1 large orange, peeled and seeded
- ¼ pound seedless red grapes
- 2 medium celery ribs, thinly sliced (1 cup)
- ½ cup chopped walnuts
  Strip of orange rind for garnish, optional
  Thin apple slices for garnish, optional

CRANBERRY DRESSING

- ¾ cup sour cream or plain low-fat yogurt
- ¾ cup canned whole-berry cranberry sauce
- 1 tablespoon grated orange rind

1. **To make salad:** In a large bowl, mix gelatin with boiling water, stirring until gelatin is completely dissolved. Stir in ginger ale and chill until thickened, about 20 minutes.

**PREP TIME: 35 MINUTES
CHILL TIME: AT LEAST 4 1/2 HR**

2. Meanwhile, chop apples and orange into ½-inch pieces. Cut the grapes in half. When gelatin is thick, fold in the apples, orange, grapes, celery, and walnuts. Transfer mixture to a lightly oiled 6-cup metal mold or glass serving bowl. Chill for at least 4 hours, until firm.

3. **To make dressing:** Meanwhile, make the dressing. In a medium bowl, mix sour cream, cranberry sauce, and orange rind until well blended. Transfer to a small serving dish, cover, and chill until ready to serve.

4. To serve, unmold the salad (see page 87) onto a serving platter. (If chilled in a glass bowl, serve directly from the bowl.) Garnish with orange rind and apple slices. Serve dressing separately to spoon over each serving. Makes about six 1-cup servings.

1 serving: 281 calories, 4 g protein, 13 g total fat (4.4 g saturated), 42 g carbohydrates, 76 mg sodium, 13 mg cholesterol, 3 g dietary fiber

FROZEN CRANBERRY SNOW

MAKES 6 SERVINGS

Between Thanksgiving and the New Year, I try to feature this elegant salad at one dinner party at least. The flavor goes splendidly with roasted turkey or goose. Other times of the year, it can be made with fruit other than cranberries such as strawberries, raspberries, or peaches—just decrease the sugar from 1 cup to ⅓ cup.

SALAD

- 2 cups fresh cranberries, picked over, rinsed, and finely chopped
- 1 cup sugar
- 2 3-ounce packages cream cheese, softened at room temperature
- 2 tablespoons mayonnaise
- 1 large navel orange
- ½ cup chopped pecans
- ½ cup heavy cream, whipped
  Orange rind strips for garnish, optional

CRANBERRY SAUCE

- 1 cup fresh cranberries
- ⅔ cup sugar
- 2 tablespoons orange liqueur or water
- 1 teaspoon grated orange rind

PREP TIME: 30 MIN
CHILL TIME: 8 HR
COOK TIME: 30 MIN
FREEZE TIME: AT LEAST 8 HR

1. **To make salad:** Finely chop cranberries. In a medium bowl, combine chopped cranberries and 1 cup sugar. Cover and chill for at least 8 hours. Drain in a colander and discard any liquid.

2. In a large bowl, beat cream cheese and mayonnaise until smooth and well blended. Peel and section orange, removing all white pith. Chop orange sections. Stir orange, drained cranberries, and pecans into cream cheese mixture. Using a rubber spatula, gently and thoroughly fold in whipped cream.

3. Spoon mixture into a 9 x 5-inch loaf pan. Cover with plastic wrap and freeze until firm, about 8 hours.

4. **To make sauce:** In a small saucepan, combine 1 cup cranberries, ⅔ cup sugar, and liqueur. Cook over low heat, stirring occasionally, until cranberries are translucent and sugar dissolves, about 30 minutes. Transfer cranberries and any liquid to a bowl. Let cool, then cover and chill until ready to serve.

5. To serve, spoon some cranberry sauce into the center of 6 short-stemmed glass dessert dishes. Place one scoop of cranberry snow over sauce. Garnish with strips of orange rind. Makes 6 servings.

1 serving: 537 calories, 4 g protein, 28 g total fat (11.9 g saturated), 71 g carbohydrates, 119 mg sodium, 61 mg cholesterol, 3 g dietary fiber

SOURCES

AMERICAN SPOON FOODS
(dried cherries, dried cranberries, and morels)
P.O. Box 566
Petoskey, MI 49770–0556
(800) 222–5886

FOREST RESOURCE CENTER
(shiitake mushrooms)
Route 2, Box 156A
Lanesboro, MN 55949
(507) 467–2437

WILD GAME INC. AND THE HERB PURVEYOR
(pheasant and duck breasts)
2315 West Huron St.
Chicago, IL 60612
(312) 278–1661

MAYTAG DAIRY FARMS
(Maytag Blue Cheese)
P.O. Box 806
Newton, IA 50208
(800) 247–2458

MOZE'S GOURMET SPECIALTIES
(wild rice)
2701 Monroe St.
Madison, WI 53711
(800) 369–7423

INDEX

A
Apple Salad, Beet and, 102
Apple Soup, Curried, 34-35
Asparagus and Red Potato Soup, Spring, 30-31
Asparagus Salad with Cilantro Dressing, Grilled Steak and, 112-113
Autumn Rabbit Soup, 52-53
Avocado Soup, 20-21

B
Bacon Dressing, Hot, 101
Balsamic Dressing, 83
Basil Dressing, 94
Bean salads
    Bean Medley, 96-97
    Seafood Salad with White Beans, 126-127
Bean soups
    Lentil Soup, 54
    Pork and Bean Soup, 59
Beef salads
    Grilled Steak and Asparagus Salad with Cilantro Dressing, 112-113
    Roast Beef Salad, 120
Beef soups,
    Beef Stock, 13
    Garden Beef Soup, 55
    Goulash Soup, 56-57
Beet and Apple Salad, 102
Berry salads
    Berry and Pretzel Salad, 137
    Frozen Cranberry Snow, 140
    Summertime Fruit Salad with Honey Lime Dressing, 134
    Wilted Greens with Chicken and Cranberries, 121
Berry soups
    Blueberry-Blackberry Soup, 69
    Sparkling Cranberry Soup, 74
    Strawberry Melon Soup, 72
Bisque, Chilled Carrot, 16-17
BLT in a Bowl with Garlic Croutons, 118-119

Blueberry-Blackberry Soup, 69
Blue Cheese Salad with Balsamic Dressing, Endive, Pear, and, 82-83
Borscht, Heartland, 25
Broccoli Salad with Sweet and Sour Raisin Dressing, 104-105
Buttermilk Soup, Cucumber, 18-19
Buttermilk Soup, Rhubarb, 68

C
Caesar Dressing, 128
Caesar Salad, Warm Shrimp, 128-129
Cantaloupe, Tomato, and Avocado Salad with Hot Chile Dressing, 135
Carrot Bisque, Chilled, 16-17
Cauliflower Soup, 29
Cheese salads and dressings
    Endive, Pear, and Blue Cheese Salad with Balsamic Dressing, 82-83
    Feta Dressing, 106
    Macaroni and Cheese Salad, 103
    Romaine Salad with Warm Cheese Dressing, 84
Cheese soups
    Twice-Baked Potato Soup, 37
    Wisconsin Cheese Chowder, 40-41
Cherry Soup, 70-71
Chicken salads
    Grilled Citrus Chicken Salad, 124
    Wilted Greens with Chicken and Cranberries, 121
Chicken soups
    Chicken Spaetzle Soup, 50
    Chicken Stock, 12
    Velvet Chicken Soup, 62
Chile Dressing, Hot, 135
Chili Clam Chowder, 63
Chilled Carrot Bisque, 16-17
Chowders
    Chili Clam Chowder, 63
    Country Corn Chowder, 22-23
    Great Lakes Fish Chowder, 43
    Ham and Sweet Potato Chowder, 58
    Salmon Chowder, 44-45

    Whitefish Chowder, 42
    Wisconsin Cheese Chowder, 40-41
Cilantro Dressing, 112
Citrus Chicken Salad, Grilled, 124
Clam Chowder, Chili, 63
Coleslaw, Karen's Garlicky and Sweet, 93
Confetti Salad, Summer, 94-95
Cooking and baking equivalents, 10
Corn and Tomato Salad, Heartland, 90-91
Corn Chowder, Country, 22-23
Cranberries
    Cranberry Dressing, 139
    Frozen Cranberry Snow, 140-141
    Sparkling Cranberry Soup, 74
    Wilted Greens with Chicken and Cranberries, 121
Cream soups
    Avocado Soup, 20-21
    Cauliflower Soup, 29
    Creamy Shiitake Mushroom Soup, 32
    Cucumber Buttermilk Soup, 18-19
    Old-Fashioned Cream of Tomato Soup, 26-27
    Roasted Garlic Cream Soup, 28
Crème Fraîche, 24-25, 25, 74, 134
    Roasted Red Pepper and Tomato Soup with Crème Fraîche Swirl, 24-25
    in Heartland Borscht, 25
    in Sparkling Cranberry Soup, 74
    in Summertime Fruit Salad with Honey Lime Dressing, 134
Croutons, Garlic, 46-47, 84, 119, 128
Cucumber Buttermilk Soup, 18-19
Cucumber Salad, Molded, 86-87
Curdling of soup, preventing, 11
Curried Apple Soup, 34-35

D
Dill Vinegar, 89
Dressings
    Balsamic Dressing, 83
    Basil Dressing, 94
    Caesar Dressing, 128
    Cilantro Dressing, 112

Cranberry Dressing, 139
Feta Dressing, 106
Fresh Herb Dressing, 127
Hazelnut Vinaigrette, 122
Herb Dressing, 123
Herb Dressing, Fresh, 127
Herb Mustard Dressing, 97
Honey-Dijon Dressing, 102
Honey-Lime Dressing, 134
Honey-Mustard Dressing, 136
Horseradish-Dill Dressing, 117
Hot Bacon Dressing, 101
Hot Chile Dressing, 135
Jalapeño Mayonnaise, 85
Mustard Vinaigrette, 119
Poppy Seed Dressing, 80
Raspberry Vinaigrette, 124
Red Wine Vinegar Dressing, 91
Salsa Dressing, 114
Specialty Vinegars, 89
Sweet and Sour Raisin Dressing, 105
Tarragon Dressing, 120
Warm Cheese Dressing, 84
Duck Salad, Grilled, 122

E
Endive, Pear, and Blue Cheese Salad with
    Balsamic Dressing, 82-83
Endive varieties, 77
Equipment for soup-making, 11
Equivalents, tables of, 10

F
Fall Fruit Salad, Mixed, 136
Farmers' Market Soup, 46-47
Feta Dressing, 106
Fiddlehead Salad, Warm, 88
Fish and shellfish salads, 108-109
    Seafood Salad with White Beans, 126-127
    Tuna and Pasta Salad, 125
    Warm Shrimp Caesar Salad, 128-129
Fish and shellfish soups
    Chili Clam Chowder, 63
    Great Lakes Fish Chowder, 43
    Salmon Chowder, 44-45
    Shrimp and Tomato Soup, 60-61
    Whitefish Chowder, 42
5-Cup Salad (Prairie Fruit Salad), 132-133
Freezing soups and stock, 11
Fresh Herb Dressing, 127
Frozen Cranberry Snow, 140-141
Fruited Spinach Salad with Poppy Seed
    Dressing, 80-81

G
Game
    Autumn Rabbit Soup, 52-53
    Grilled Duck Salad, 122
    Pheasant Soup, 48-49
Garden Beef Soup, 55
Garlic Cream Soup, Roasted, 28
Garlic Croutons
    BLT in a Bowl with, 118-119

Farmers' Market Soup with, 46-47
    Romaine Salad with Warm Cheese
        Dressing, 84
    Warm Shrimp Caesar Salad, 128-129
Garlicky and Sweet Coleslaw, Karen's, 93
Garnishes
    Crème Fraîche, 24-25, 25, 74, 134
    Garlic Croutons, 46-47, 84, 119, 128
    Spicy Hazelnuts, 20-21, 122
Gelatin salads. *See Molded salads*
German Potato Salad with Grilled
    Sausages, Hot, 110-111
Goulash Soup, 56-57
Grain salads
    Mixed Grain Salad with
        Feta Dressing, 106-107
    North Woods Wild Rice Salad, 100
    Smoked Turkey Salad, 123
Great Lakes Fish Chowder, 43
Greens, salad, 76-77
Green salads, 78-79
    Endive, Pear, and Blue Cheese Salad
        with Balsamic Dressing, 82-83
    Fruited Spinach Salad with Poppy Seed
        Dressing, 80-81
    Kansas Layered 24-Hour Salad, 98
    Romaine Salad with Warm Cheese
        Dressing, 84
    Warm Shrimp Caesar Salad, 128-129
    Wilted Greens with Chicken and
        Cranberries, 121
Grilled Citrus Chicken Salad, 124
Grilled Duck Salad, 122
Grilled Sausages, Hot German Potato
    Salad with, 110-111
Grilled Steak and Asparagus Salad with
    Cilantro Dressing, 112-113
Grilled Vegetable Salad, Warm, 92

H
Ham and Pea Salad with Fresh Dill,
    Potato, 116-117
Ham and Sweet Potato
    Chowder, 58
Hazelnuts, Spicy, 20-21, 122
Hazelnut Vinaigrette, 122
Heartland Borscht, 25
Heartland Summer Corn and Tomato
    Salad, 90-91
Herb Dressing, 123
Herb Dressing, Fresh, 127
Herb Mustard Dressing, 97
Honey-Dijon Dressing, 102
Honey-Mustard Dressing, 136
Horseradish-Dill Dressing, 117
Hot Bacon Dressing, 101
Hot Chile Dressing, 135
Hot German Potato Salad with
    Grilled Sausages, 110-111

I
Italian Salad Vinegar, 89

J
Jalapeño Mayonnaise, 85

K
Kansas Layered 24-Hour Salad, 98
Karen's Garlicky and Sweet Coleslaw, 93

L
Layered 24-Hour Salad, Kansas, 98
Lemon-Lime Mold, Tangy, 138
Lentil Soup, 54
Lettuce varieties, 77

M
Macaroni salads. *See also Pasta salads*
    Macaroni and Cheese Salad, 103
Mayonnaise, Jalapeño, 85
Maytag blue cheese, 94
Measurement equivalents, liquid and dry,
    10
Meat salads, 108-109. *See also Beef salads;*
    Fish and shellfish salads; Pork salads;
    Poultry salads
Melon Soup, Strawberry, 72
Metric conversion chart, 10
Micro-cooked soups
    Chili Clam Chowder, 63
    Shrimp and Tomato Soup, 60-61
    Spicy Sausage Soup, 64-65
    Velvet Chicken Soup, 62
Microwave cooking times, 61
Minestrone, Turkey, 51
Mixed Fall Fruit Salad, 136
Mixed Grain Salad with Feta Dressing,
    106-107
Molded salads
    Molded Cucumber Salad, 86-87
    Molded Waldorf Salad with Cranberry
        Dressing, 139
    Tangy Lemon-Lime Mold, 138
    unmolding tips, 87
Mushroom Soup, Creamy Shiitake, 32
Mustard Dressing, Herb, 97
Mustard Vinaigrette, 119

N
North Woods Wild Rice Salad, 100

O
Old-Fashioned Cream of Tomato Soup,
    26- 27
Old-Fashioned Red Potato Salad, 99
Onion Soup, Roasted, 33
Opal Basil Vinegar, 89

P
Party menus, main dish soups and, 39
Pasta salads
    Macaroni and Cheese Salad, 103
    Summer Confetti Salad, 94-95
    Tuna and Pasta Salad, 125
Peaches, in Grilled Duck Salad, 122
Peach Soup, 73
Pear and Blue Cheese Salad with
    Balsamic Dressing, Endive, 82-83
Persimmons, 136

Pheasant Soup, 48-49
Pomegranate seeding tips, 102
Poppy Seed Dressing, 80
Pork salads
  BLT in a Bowl with Garlic Croutons,
    118-119
  Hot German Potato Salad with
    Grilled Sausages, 110-111
  Potato, Ham, and Pea Salad with
    Fresh Dill, 116-117
  Tortilla Taco Salad, 114-115
Pork Soups
  Ham and Sweet Potato
    Chowder, 58
  Pork and Bean Soup, 59
  Spicy Sausage Soup, 64-65
Potato salads
  Hot German Potato Salad with
    Grilled Sausages, 110-111
  Old-Fashioned Red Potato Salad, 99
  Potato, Ham, and Pea Salad with
    Fresh Dill, 116-117
Potato soups
  Ham and Sweet Potato Chowder, 58
  Spring Asparagus and Red Potato Soup,
    30-31
  Twice-Baked Potato Soup, 37
Poultry Salad, 108-109
  Grilled Citrus Chicken Salad, 124
  Grilled Duck Salad, 122
  Smoked Turkey Salad, 123
  Wilted Greens with Chicken and
    Cranberries, 121
Poultry soups
  Chicken Stock, 12
  Chicken Spaetzle Soup, 50
  Pheasant Soup, 48-49
  Turkey Minestrone, 51
  Velvet Chicken Soup, 62
Prairie Fruit Salad, 132-133
Pretzel Salad, Berry and, 137
Pumpkin Soup, 36

Q
Quinoa, 106
R
Rabbit Soup, Autumn, 52-53
Raisin Dressing, Sweet and Sour, 105
Raspberry Thyme Vinegar, 89
Red Pepper and Tomato Soup with
  Crème Fraîche Swirl, Roasted, 24-25
Red Potato Salad, Old-Fashioned, 99
Red Potato Soup, Spring Asparagus and,
  30-31
Red Wine Vinegar Dressing, 91
Rhubarb Buttermilk Soup, 68
Rice salads
  North Woods Wild Rice Salad, 100
  Smoked Turkey Salad, 123
Roasted Garlic Cream Soup, 28
Roasted Onion Soup, 33

Roasted Red Pepper and Tomato Soup
  with Crème Fraîche Swirl, 24-25
Romaine Salad with Warm Cheese
  Dressing, 84
Root Vegetable Salad, Warm, 101
Rosemary Vinegar, 89
S
Salad greens, 77
Salmon Chowder, 44-45
Salsa Dressing, 114-115
Sausages
  Hot German Potato Salad with
    Grilled Sausages, 110-111
  Spicy Sausage Soup, 64-65
Seafood Salad, 108-109
  Seafood Salad with White Beans,
    126-127
  Tuna and Pasta Salad, 125
  Warm Shrimp Caesar Salad, 128-129
Seafood soups. *See Fish and shellfish soups*
Serving suggestions for soups, 11, 15
Shellfish salads.
  See fish and shellfish salads
Shellfish soups.
  See fish and shellfish soups
Shiitake Mushroom Soup, Creamy, 32
Shrimp and Tomato Soup, 60-61
Shrimp Caesar Salad, Warm, 128-129
Smoked Turkey Salad, 123
Spaetzle Chicken Soup, 50
Sparkling Cranberry Soup, 74-75
Specialty Vinegars, 89
Spicy Hazelnuts
  Avocado Soup with, 20-21
  Grilled Duck Salad with, 122
Spicy Sausage Soup, 64-65
Spinach Salad with
  Poppy Seed Dressing, Fruited, 80-81
Spring Asparagus and Red Potato Soup,
  30-31
Steak and Asparagus Salad with
  Cilantro Dressing, Grilled, 112-113
Stock
  Beef Stock, 13
  Chicken Stock, 12
  commercial and homemade, 11
Strawberry Melon Soup, 72
Summer Confetti Salad, 94-95
Summertime Fruit Salad with
  Honey-Lime Dressing, 134
Sweet and Sour Raisin Dressing, 105
Sweet Potato Chowder, Ham and, 58
T
Taco Salad, Tortilla, 114-115
Tangy Lemon-Lime Mold, 138
Tarragon Dressing, 120
Tarragon Vinegar, 89
Temperature equivalents, 10
Tex-Mex Vinegar, 89
Thyme and Rosemary Vinegar, 89

Tomato salads
  Cantaloupe, Tomato, and Avocado Salad
    with Hot Chile Dressing, 135
  Heartland Summer Corn and
    Tomato Salad, 90-91
  Tomato Salad with Jalapeño
    Mayonnaise, 85
Tomato soups
  Old-Fashioned Cream of
    Tomato Soup, 26-27
  Roasted Red Pepper and Tomato Soup
    with Crème Fraîche Swirl, 24-25
  Shrimp and Tomato Soup, 60-61
Tortilla Shells, 114-115
Tortilla Taco Salad, 114-115
Tuna and Pasta Salad, 125
Turkey Minestrone, 51
Turkey Salad, Smoked, 123
24-Hour Salad, Kansas Layered, 98
Twice-Baked Potato Soup, 37
V
Vegetable soups. *See also specific vegetables*
  Chicken Spaetzle Soup, 50
  Farmers' Market Soup, 46-47
  Garden Beef Soup, 55
  Vegetables as soup "bowls", 15
Velvet Chicken Soup, 62
Vinaigrette dressings
  Hazelnut Vinaigrette, 122
  Mustard Vinaigrette, 119
  Raspberry Vinaigrette, 124
  Red Wine Vinegar Dressing, 91
  Walnut Oil Vinaigrette, 125
Vinegars, Specialty, 89
W
Waldorf Salad with Cranberry Dressing,
  Molded, 139
Walnut Oil Vinaigrette, 125
Warm Cheese Dressing, 84
Warm Fiddlehead Salad, 88
Warm Grilled Vegetable Salad, 92
Warm Root Vegetable Salad, 101
Warm Shrimp Caesar Salad, 128-129
White Beans, Seafood Salad with,
  126-127
Whitefish Chowder, 42
Wild Rice Salad, North Woods, 100
Wilted Greens with Chicken and
  Cranberries, 121
Wisconsin Cheese Chowder, 40-41